SLAYING
THE
GIANTS
IN YOUR LIFE

You Can Win the Battle and
Live Victoriously

David Jeremiah

with Dr. David Jeremiah

Edited by Jordan Davis

Unless otherwise indicated, Scripture verses quoted are taken from the NEW KING JAMES VERSION.

Printed in the United States of America.

CONTENTS

ABOUT
DR. DAVID JEREMIAH
AND TURNING POINT

D r. David Jeremiah is the founder of Turning Point, a ministry committed to providing Christians with sound Bible teaching relevant to today's changing times through radio and television broadcasts, audio series, books, and live events. Dr. Jeremiah's common-sense teaching on topics such as family, prayer, worship, angels, and biblical prophecy forms the foundation of Turning Point.

David and his wife, Donna, reside in El Cajon, California, where he serves as the senior pastor of Shadow Mountain Community Church. David and Donna have four children and twelve grandchildren.

In 1982, Dr. Jeremiah brought the same solid teaching to San Diego television that he shares weekly with his congregation. Shortly thereafter, Turning Point expanded its ministry to radio. Dr. Jeremiah's inspiring messages can now be heard worldwide on radio, television, and the Internet.

Because Dr. Jeremiah desires to know his listening audience, he travels nationwide holding ministry events that touch the hearts and lives of many people. According to Dr. Jeremiah, "At some point in time, everyone reaches a turning point; and for every person, that moment is unique, an experience to hold onto forever. There's so much changing in today's world that sometimes it's difficult to choose the right path. Turning Point offers people an understanding of God's Word as well as the opportunity to make a difference in their lives."

Dr. Jeremiah has authored numerous books, including *Escape the Coming Night* (Revelation), *The Handwriting on the Wall* (Daniel), *Overcoming Loneliness, God in You* (Holy Spirit), *When Your World Falls Apart, 31 Days to Happiness—Searching for Heaven on Earth, Captured by Grace, What in the World Is Going On?, I Never Thought I'd See the Day!, Agents of the Apocalypse, RESET—Ten Steps to Spiritual Renewal, Ten Questions Christians Are Asking, A Life Beyond Amazing, Perhaps Today,* and *Overcomer.*

How to Use This
Study Guide

The purpose of this Turning Point study guide is to reinforce Dr. David Jeremiah's dynamic, in-depth teaching and to aid the reader in applying biblical truth to his or her daily life. This study guide is designed to be used in conjunction with Dr. Jeremiah's *Slaying the Giants in Your Life* audio series, but it may also be used by itself for personal or group study.

Structure of the Lessons

Each lesson is based on one of the messages in the *Slaying the Giants in Your Life* compact disc series and focuses on specific passages in the Bible. Each lesson is composed of the following elements:

- *Outline*

The outline at the beginning of the lesson gives a clear, concise picture of the topic being studied and provides a helpful framework for readers as they listen to Dr. Jeremiah's teaching.

- *Overview*

The overview summarizes Dr. Jeremiah's teaching on the passage being studied in the lesson. Readers should refer to the Scripture passages in their own Bibles as they study the overview. Unless otherwise indicated, Scripture verses quoted are taken from the New King James Version.

- *Personal and Group Application Questions*

This section contains a variety of questions designed to help readers dig deeper into the lesson and the Scriptures, and to apply the lesson to their daily lives. For Bible study groups or Sunday school classes, these questions will provide a springboard for group discussion and interaction.

- *Did You Know?*

This section presents a fascinating fact, historical note, or insight that adds a point of interest to the preceding lesson.

Personal Study

Thank you for selecting *Slaying the Giants in Your Life* for your current study. The lessons in this study guide were created to help you gain fresh insights into God's Word and develop new perspectives on topics you may have previously studied. Each lesson is designed to challenge your thinking, and help you grow in your knowledge of Christ. During your study, it is our prayer that you will discover how biblical truth affects every aspect of your life and your relationship with Christ will be strengthened.

When you commit to completing this study guide, try to set apart a time, daily or weekly, to read through the lessons without distraction. Have your Bible nearby when you read the study guide, so you're ready to look up verses if you need to. If you want to use a notebook to write down your thoughts, be sure to have that handy as well. Take your time to think through and answer the questions. If you plan on reading the study guide with a small group, be sure to read ahead and be prepared to take part in the weekly discussions.

Leader's Guide

Thank you for your commitment to lead a group through *Slaying the Giants in Your Life*. Being a leader has its own rewards. You may discover that your walk with the Lord deepens through this experience. Throughout the study guide, your group will explore new topics and review study questions that encourage thought-provoking group discussion.

The lessons in this study guide are suitable for Sunday school classes, small-group studies, elective Bible studies, or home Bible study groups. Each lesson is structured to provoke thought and help you grow in your knowledge and understanding of God. There are multiple components in this section that can help you structure your lessons and discussion time, so make sure you read and consider each one.

Before You Begin

Before you begin each meeting, make sure you and your group are well-versed with the content of the chapter. Every person should have his or her own study guide so they can follow along and write in the study guide if need be. When possible, the study guide should be used with the corresponding compact disc series. You may wish to assign the study guide lesson as homework prior to the meeting of the group and then use the meeting time to listen to the CD and discuss the lesson.

To ensure that everyone has a chance to participate in the discussion, the ideal size for a group is around eight to ten people. If there are more than ten people, try to break up the bigger group into smaller subgroups. Make sure the members are committed to participating each week, as this will help create stability and help you better prepare the structure of the meeting.

At the beginning of the study each week, start the session with a question to challenge group members to think about the issues you will be discussing. The members can answer briefly, but the goal is to have an idea in their mind as you go over the lesson. This allows the group members to become engaged and ready to interact with the group.

After reviewing the lesson, try to initiate a free-flowing discussion. Invite group members to bring questions and insights they may have discovered to the next meeting, especially if they were unsure of the meaning of some parts of the lesson. Be prepared to discuss how biblical truth applies to the world we live in today.

Weekly Preparation

As the group leader, here are a few things you can do to prepare for each meeting:

- Choose whether or not you will play the CD message during your small group session.

  If you decide to play the CD message from Dr. Jeremiah as part of the meeting, you will need to adjust the group time accordingly.

- Make sure you are thoroughly familiar with the material in the lesson.

  Make sure you understand the content of the lesson so you know how to structure group time and you are prepared to lead group discussion.

- Decide, ahead of time, which questions you plan to discuss.

  Depending on how much time you have each week, you may not be able to reflect on every question. Select specific questions which you feel will evoke the best discussion.

- Take prayer requests.

  At the end of your discussion, take prayer requests from your group members and pray for each other.

Structuring the Discussion Time

If you need help in organizing your time when planning your group Bible study, here are two schedules, for sixty minutes and ninety minutes, which can give you a structure for the lesson:

Option 1 (Listen to Audio CD)	60 Minutes	90 Minutes
Welcome: Members arrive and get settled.	N/A	5 minutes
Getting Started Question: Prepares the group for interacting with one another.	Welcome and Getting Started 5 minutes	15 minutes
Message: Listen to the audio CD.	40 minutes	40 minutes
Discussion: Discuss group study questions.	10 minutes	25 minutes
Prayer and Application: Final application for the week and prayer before dismissal.	5 minutes	5 minutes

Option 2 (No Audio CD)	60 Minutes	90 Minutes
Welcome: Members arrive and get settled.	5 minutes	10 minutes
Getting Started Question: Prepares the group for interacting with one another.	10 minutes	10 minutes
Message: Review the lesson.	15 minutes	25 minutes
Discussion: Discuss group study questions.	25 minutes	35 minutes
Prayer and Application: Final application for the week and prayer before dismissal.	5 minutes	10 minutes

As the group leader, it is up to you to keep track of the time and keep things moving along according to your schedule. If your group is having a good discussion, don't feel the need to stop and move on to the next question. Remember, the purpose is to pull together ideas, and share unique insights on the lesson. Make time each week to discuss how to apply these truths to living for Christ today.

The purpose of discussion is for everyone to participate, but don't be concerned if certain group members are more quiet—they may be internally reflecting on the questions and need time to process their ideas before they can share them.

Group Dynamics

Leading a group study can be a rewarding experience for you and your group members—but that doesn't mean there won't be challenges. Certain members may feel uncomfortable discussing topics that they consider very personal, and might be afraid of being called on. Some members might have disagreements on specific issues. To help prevent these scenarios, consider the following ground rules:

- If someone has a question that may seem off topic, suggest that it is discussed at another time, or ask the group if they are okay with addressing that topic.

- If someone asks a question you don't know the answer to, confess that you don't know and move on. If you feel comfortable, invite other group members to give their opinions, or share their comments based on personal experience.

- If you feel like a couple of people are talking much more than others, direct questions to people who may not have shared yet. You could even ask the more dominating members to help draw out the quiet ones.

- When there is a disagreement, encourage the group members to process the matter in love. Invite members from opposing sides to evaluate their opinions and consider the ideas of the other members. Lead the group through Scripture that addresses the topic, and look for common ground.

When issues arise, remind your group to think of Scripture: "Love one another" (John 13:34), "If it is possible, as much as depends on you, live peaceably with all men" (Romans 12:18), and "Be quick to listen, slow to speak and slow to become angry" (James 1:19, NIV).

For Continuing Study

For a complete listing of Dr. Jeremiah's materials for personal and group study call 1-800-947-1993, go online to www.DavidJeremiah.org, or write to Turning Point, P.O. Box 3838, San Diego, CA 92163.

Dr. Jeremiah's *Turning Point* program is currently heard or viewed around the world on radio, television, and the Internet in English. *Momento Decisivo*, the Spanish translation of Dr. Jeremiah's messages, can be heard on radio in every Spanish speaking country in the world. The television broadcast is also broadcast by satellite throughout the Middle East with Arabic subtitles.

Contact Turning Point for radio and television program times and stations in your area, or visit our website at www.DavidJeremiah.org/stationlocator.

SLAYING THE GIANTS IN YOUR LIFE

With the exponential advances in technology that seem to present themselves daily, the devices in our lives that we use to function have only become smaller and more advanced in their capabilities. On a smartphone that fits in the palm of our hand, we can stay in constant communication with others through its phone and Internet capacities and have instant access to thousands of our favorite songs. And with a tablet, we can download endless books onto a small screen and no longer have to lug various tomes around by hand. Life has never been more convenient.

Life has also never been more complicated. Even though the toys and gadgets that we surround ourselves with have gotten smaller, our problems seem to have only gotten bigger. In an era where we can be reached at a moment's notice anywhere in the world, loneliness has never been greater. Moreover, with instantaneous access to news and current events, there has never been a greater opportunity to worry. And with all that the world has to offer available at the simple click of a button, temptation has never been a more looming issue for the believer.

So how do we tackle these ancient giants who still menace God's people in a modern world? Let's look to the example of David, who as a mere shepherd boy defeated a looming giant of his own—Goliath.

David possessed an attitude of victory before the battle even began. In 1 Samuel 17:32, he said of Goliath, "Let no man's heart fail because of him." He then went to battle this giant without the aid of armor, sword, or shield. What was the source of such a great confidence? It was not in himself and his own abilities, for David had no business taking on a giant on his own. But he knew that he didn't have to rely on his own strength; he knew that the battle was the Lord's, and that He would deliver Goliath into his hands (1 Samuel 17:47).

So how does that help us defeat giants like guilt, failure, and jealousy in our own lives? Well, David did not rely on his own strength, and neither should we. And unlike David, we have access to a wealth of knowledge and encouragement and power; we have the Word of God! And heading into battles with giants that are so threatening and intimidating, it is good to know that "the word of God is living and powerful, and sharper than any two-edged sword" (Hebrews 4:12). We are not weak—we are empowered!

Slaying the Giants in Your Life will help you to do exactly that. Together, we will identify and define each giant that can discourage the Christian in their walk, and then we will use Scripture to defeat its hazardous lies. Through prayer, study, and the work of the Holy Spirit, we can face down the most daunting giants with the power of God. And in doing so, we can share in the encouraging words of Moses, that "the Lord, He is the One who goes before you. He will be with you, He will not leave you nor forsake you; do not fear nor be dismayed" (Deuteronomy 31:8).

SLAYING THE GIANT OF FEAR

Deuteronomy 1:19-40

In this lesson we learn how to overcome the debilitating effects of fear.

OUTLINE

The opposite of faith is not unbelief—it is fear. That's because both faith and fear are focused on the future, the realm of the unknown. Fear cancels out faith because it can freeze us in our tracks. Fear is overcome by faith in the God who knows the future.

I. **Fear Disregards God's Plan**

II. **Fear Distorts God's Purposes**

III. **Fear Discourages God's People**

IV. **Fear Disbelieves God's Promises**

V. **Fear Disobeys God's Principles**

VI. **Fear Demands a Biblical Response**
    A. Confront Your Fear Honestly
    B. Confess Your Fear as Sin
    C. Claim God's Promises of Protection
    D. Cultivate a Closer Relationship With God
    E. Commit Your Life to Jesus Christ

This series of studies is not about the kinds of giants we read about in the Old Testament—giants like Goliath who stood more than nine feet tall. Instead, we're going to talk about another breed of giants which can be every bit as threatening to our well being: spiritual giants that invade our lives and seek to destroy the work of God in us.

The first of these giants we will study is the giant of fear. Many people have phobias—those irrational roadblocks that keep them from doing things they want to do. Some people are afraid of heights, some of open spaces, some of airplanes. There are more than one hundred different phobias, and more than ten percent of the population suffers from one or more of them. But those phobias are not what we'll be studying in this series.

We will look at the spirit of fear that can take over our life and dominate us in a way God never intended. Fear is not always a bad thing. God uses fear to protect us—to keep us from doing things which might hurt us. But when fear becomes a permanent condition, it can immobilize us and bring our entire life to a standstill.

Everyone experiences fear at different times. I experience fear at times when I have to stand and speak in front of a large crowd. Every parent has experienced fear when his or her children have been injured or thrust into new situations for which they are not prepared. And some of us have experienced fear when we are told that we have a serious disease. Ideally, those fears come and go; they don't dominate our lives. It's when fear takes over that we know there is a giant that needs to be conquered.

We see fear in understandable circumstances in Scripture. When the disciples were on the Sea of Galilee during a fierce storm, they were afraid. When the Israelites were accosted by the Philistine giant, Goliath, they were afraid. But the Old Testament story which best illustrates how to deal with fear is the story of the twelve spies who left Kadesh Barnea to spy out the Promised Land of Canaan. That story is told initially in Numbers 13–14, but it is repeated in a condensed version in Deuteronomy 1:19-40.

To set the stage, Israel has been freed from slavery in Egypt and is approaching the Promised Land under Moses' leadership. Before taking the whole nation in, Moses sends twelve men into the land to check it out—to see how formidable the inhabitants were, how well the cities were fortified, and how fertile the land was. When we see the response of some of the spies upon their return, we learn that fear has not changed in several thousand years.

FEAR DISREGARDS GOD'S PLAN

Verses 19-21 of Deuteronomy 1 clearly indicate that it was God's plan for the Israelites to go up and possess the land of Canaan. Verse 21 clearly reveals what would stand in their way to keep them from fulfilling God's plan—fear and discouragement. And that is exactly what controlled the people after hearing a negative report from ten of the spies.

Fear took hold of their lives, and they couldn't believe that God had actually brought them to the place of their inheritance and their blessing. Fear will keep you from experiencing God's plan in your life. We have an inheritance today just as the Israelites did in their day. Our inheritance is just as much the plan of God as was theirs. And we have just as clear a warning from the apostle Paul as Israel had from Moses—a warning about fear: "God has not given us a spirit of fear, but of power and of love and of a sound mind"(2 Timothy 1:7). God has not created us to be creatures dominated by fear. He has given us the principle of faith upon which to live. If we choose to live in fear, we are disregarding God's plan for our life.

The same principle is given by Paul in the book of Romans: "For you did not receive the spirit of bondage again to fear, but you received the Spirit of adoption by whom we cry out, 'Abba, Father'" (Romans 8:15). God's plan for us, His desire for us, is that we live above fear, that we walk in the power of His love.

FEAR DISTORTS GOD'S PURPOSES

When fear dominates our life, everything gets out of perspective; everything gets distorted. Ten of the twelve spies who returned to Kadesh Barnea brought back a totally distorted picture of what the Promised Land was really like. Their skewed report is found in verses 27-28. They came back and reported that the Promised Land was filled with Anakim, or giants. There were giants in the land of Canaan in those days (remember Goliath?), but not every person in Canaan was a giant. Their fear caused them to see one thing and report another. They saw great cities which were well fortified, and they concluded that they would never be able to take them. In fact, their fear so totally distorted their thinking that they decided the only reason God had led them to Canaan was to destroy them!

You may think, *That is the most irrational thought you could ever have of God!* But when fear begins to control your life, you don't think correctly; rationality goes out the window. If you choose to let fear control your thinking, you will have a distorted view of the situation you are in and of life in general. Everything will be totally out of perspective. You will think God has brought you into a terrible situation just to do you harm.

Fear Discourages God's People

Not only does fear disregard God's plan and distort God's purposes, but it also discourages God's people. The kind of fear that controls is highly contagious—a communicable sin. Think of the situation in Israel at Kadesh Barnea. Ten men out of twelve came back from Canaan controlled by fear, and those ten men determined the destiny of the rest of the entire nation for the next forty years. Their words of fear so infected the rest of the people that the entire nation became fearful of going into the land God had promised. The fearful words of ten people turned the fortunes of an entire nation.

Somebody said that when the spies came back from the land of Canaan, they not only talked about the giants they saw, they brought one of the giants back with them—the giant of fear. And that giant walked into Israel's camp and destroyed everything that was in the heart of the whole nation. Fear like this is akin to someone yelling, "Fire!" in the midst of a crowded theatre. Without any knowledge of the facts, panic sets in and causes a stampede among hundreds of people. The entire landscape changes when one or more people are consumed by fear.

Fear Disbelieves God's Promises

You would think that when Israel stood on the threshold of the Promised Land and faced a new set of challenges, they would have trusted God to see them through. Wasn't He the God who worked mighty miracles for them in Egypt? Moses outlined in verses 29-33 what God had done for Israel in the past and how, on the basis of His past promise keeping, He would keep His promises to deliver Israel into the land of milk and honey. But instead, fear caused Israel to disbelieve the promises of God.

Think of all the things God had done for them: the plagues, the parting of the Red Sea, the giving of the Law, the provision of water and food in the wilderness, defeating their enemies on the way, guiding them by a pillar of fire and a cloud. God carried Israel through the wilderness as a father carries a child. Shouldn't Israel, on the basis of all those demonstrations of God's power, have trusted Him one more time? I have found in my own walk with the Lord that each new test must be approached with new faith. We cannot live on yesterday's faith. Many Christians don't realize that they can trust God ten times in a row and then disbelieve Him the eleventh time if they allow fear to set in. Yielding to fear will lead to disbelieving the promises of God.

FEAR DISOBEYS GOD'S PRINCIPLES

When we don't believe, we usually don't obey. Verse 26 documents that Israel rebelled against the command of the Lord. This may sound a bit harsh, but I believe it to be true: Fear is disobeying God. Many, many times in the Bible we are told, "Fear not," or, "Do not be afraid." Now, if we are told by God not to fear, and we choose to live in fear, what are we doing? We are disobeying God.

Because the people did not obey God, they did not go up into the land and receive from God what He had promised to give them. The entire generation of those adults who succumbed to the fear of the ten spies was kept from going up and receiving their inheritance in the land. That generation spent the next forty years wandering in the wilderness, slowly dying off, until their children's generation was of adult age. The only two people allowed to go into the land from the disobedient generation were Joshua and Caleb, the two spies who wanted the people to trust God for victory in the Promised Land.

When fear grips our lives, it ultimately destroys everything God wants to do in and through us. I have known people to whom God has given a vision, a direction for life and ministry, but who failed to follow through with God because of fear. As a result, their lives became rambling, meaningless journeys instead of focused, purposeful missions. Fear can steal the very thing God wants to give us.

What do we do when fear is knocking on the door of our heart? How do we keep it from taking control? Five principles will protect you from being controlled by fear.

FEAR DEMANDS A BIBLICAL RESPONSE

Confront Your Fear Honestly

Fear doesn't just decide to act nice and leave you alone. You have to confront it to get rid of it. You must discover what it is that is giving fear an invitation to take up residence in your life and face it honestly. If you don't know what it is, ask God in prayer. Get counsel from a trusted friend or pastor. You can't get rid of what you can't identify.

In the nineties, *Moody Monthly* magazine had a fascinating story about a Canadian family who was growing fearful about the likelihood of another world war. They wanted to move to a location in the world where peace would be assured. So they moved to the British-controlled Falkland Islands off the coast of Argentina in March 1982. Five days later, the Argentine army invaded the Falkland Islands, and the family found themselves in the middle of a war. That's how fear is. It will follow you wherever you go unless you confront it.

Confess Your Fear as Sin

I have touched on this already—if God says "Fear not," and we fear, we are disobeying God. And disobeying God is sin. You may think it is impossible to be able to command your feelings, to tell your feelings to "fear not." You may not be able to command your feelings, but you can command your will to obey the voice of the Lord and fill your life with His truth. Psalm 34:4 says, "I sought the Lord, and He heard me, and delivered me from all my fears." Where our will goes, our feelings follow. If we seek the Lord, obey the Lord, dwell in the Lord, meditate on the Lord's Word, we will find our feelings—including our feelings of fear—following closely behind. Too many people try to get rid of fear without recognizing it and confessing it as sin. What God has forgiven and removed will not have dominion over you.

Claim God's Promises of Protection

If I found myself overcome by fear, here is what I would do. I would take a stack of index cards and fill them with verses from the Personal and Group Questions section of this lesson (plus as many other verses on fear as I could locate). Put one verse on each card; then put the cards in places where you will see them all day long: on your car visor or dashboard, on the bathroom mirror, on the kitchen counter, on your desk at work, in your purse or wallet, in a coat pocket. Everywhere you go, take the Word of God with you to remind you of the truth about fear.

Wherever you are, when the spirit of fear begins to intimidate you, you will have the truth of God near at hand. Instead of allowing your mind to be filled with fearful lies, fill it with the Word of God. Tell the enemy when he begins whispering to you about fear, "Forget it. I have a word from God that says, 'Fear not!'"

Cultivate a Closer Relationship With God

Before dismissing this as elementary, think carefully with me. What was it about the two of the twelve spies who weren't fearful, the two who believed God would help them take the land? We get a clear picture of them from three passages of Scripture: Deuteronomy 1:36; Numbers 14:24; 32:12. To summarize, all three of these passages say that Joshua and Caleb followed the Lord. This was the difference between the two who were courageous and the ten who were fearful. They had a relationship with God that was the dominant force in their lives. As a result, there was no room for fear. When they saw giants and walled cities, they said, "Our God can handle this. What's to fear?" Where the others saw obstacles, Joshua and Caleb saw God.

God's perfect love casts out fear (1 John 4:18). Just as a parent showers a fearful child with love and protection when he or she is frightened, so God enfolds us in His loving arms and casts out fear.

Commit Your Life to Jesus Christ

The greatest fear anyone could have is the fear of death (Hebrews 2:14-15). It only stands to reason that if the greatest fear is conquered, all lesser fears could be conquered as well. There is only one sure way to conquer the fear of death, and that is by accepting the gift of eternal life offered by Jesus Christ. If you are a Christian, certain of your eternal life, you have already conquered the greatest fear. No other fear should concern you. If you are not a Christian, and live not only in fear of death but of other things as well, I invite you to begin this series of lessons by accepting God's gift of love for you, Jesus Christ. Remember: His perfect love casts out all fear.

PERSONAL QUESTIONS

1. Turn to Deuteronomy 1:19-40.

   a. What was God's plan for the Israelites in verse 21?

   b. How many men went to search out the land? (verse 23) What was their feedback when reporting back? (verses 26-28)

   c. What does 2 Timothy 1:7 remind us of?

   d. Why do you think ten of the twelve were so afraid? What happened to their thought process so that they believed God led them to Canaan to destroy them?

   e. Is fear a sin? Why or why not? What does God say about fear throughout the Bible?

   f. What did Moses remind the Israelites of in verses 29-33? Had God followed through on His promises in the past?

   g. As a reminder not to fear in the future, list a few ways God has provided for you in the past.

   h. Rather than giving in to fear, what is one way you can "fear not," according to Psalm 34:4?

2. Read Hebrews 2:14-15.

   a. Christ became flesh and blood so He could destroy whom and what? (verse 14)

   b. Because of His sacrifice, He released us from the fear of what? (verse 15)

   c. If we have been released from the fear of death, how then should we live?

1. Review Deuteronomy 1:19-40.

   a. Discuss God's plan for Israel as mentioned in verses 20-21. What command is given at the end of verse 21?

   b. Why were ten of the twelve spies so fearful when they returned from the land? (verses 26-28)

   c. Recall and discuss a time in your life when fear distorted your thinking about God's purpose.

   d. How did Moses reassure the Israelites in verses 29-33? Discuss the ways in which God provided for them in the past.

   e. Because of their fear and resistance, how many years did the Israelites spend wandering in the wilderness?

2. Discuss the five principles that will protect us from being controlled by fear.

   a. Which two men were allowed into the Promised Land? For what reason? (See Deuteronomy 1:36-38; Numbers 14:24; Numbers 32:12.)

b. Why is it necessary to confess our fears as sin to the Lord? Is there a fear you need to confess? If comfortable, share with the group.

c. What casts out fear? (1 John 4:18) If the greatest fear has already been conquered (Hebrews 2:14-15), discuss why no other fear should concern us as Christians.

DID YOU KNOW?

There is one kind of fear that is permitted and even promoted throughout the Bible—the fear of God. The word "fear" when used in such contexts denotes reverence, wonder, and awe for the Lord. God is holy and needs to be approached with a spirit of humility. He is not to be taken or approached lightly. And we can see examples of this holy and righteous fear throughout Scripture, from Abraham willingly offering Isaac as a sacrifice (Genesis 22:12) to the worship of God before His throne (Revelation 19:5).

SLAYING THE GIANT OF DISCOURAGEMENT

Nehemiah 4

In this lesson we learn how to recognize and respond to discouragement.

OUTLINE

The prefix "dis-" suggests that discouragement is the absence of courage. To be discouraged means not to approach life with courage; to lose sight of the victory that is ours. Looking at life from God's perspective helps to regain our courage for living.

I. **Recognizing Discouragement**
   A. Discouragement Factor Number One: Fatigue
   B. Discouragement Factor Number Two: Frustration
   C. Discouragement Factor Number Three: Failure
   D. Discouragement Factor Number Four: Fear

II. **Responding to Discouragement**
   A. Cry Out to God
   B. Continue the Work God Has Given You to Do
   C. Concentrate on the Big Picture
   D. Claim the Encouragement of God's Promises
   E. Carry Somebody Else's Burden

OVERVIEW

In this lesson we encounter another of the spiritual giants whose shadow falls across the landscape of the Church—the giant of discouragement. Because the Bible is filled with stories about real people facing real challenges—people like you and me—we encounter discouragement in Scripture. Thankfully, God directed the writing down of stories that we can relate to right where we live. Stories like Nehemiah's give us hope that, while discouragement may come our way, we do not have to live with it. We can learn to overcome the giant of discouragement.

Here's the setting for what the Bible tells us of the life of Nehemiah. Seventy years before we meet him, Israel had been conquered by Babylon and taken into captivity. Then Babylon was conquered by Persia. The Persian King Cyrus gave the Jewish captives permission to return to their homeland and rebuild it. First to return was Zerubbabel who led a group to begin rebuilding the temple. Next came a priest by the name of Ezra and an administrator named Nehemiah.

As a priest, Ezra set about to build up the hearts of the returned captives, while Nehemiah focused on rebuilding Jerusalem's walls. By the time we get to Nehemiah 4, we find Nehemiah has organized the people into efficient crews of laborers who are hard at work on the walls. They were about halfway finished rebuilding the walls when opposition to the project surfaced (Nehemiah 4:7). Two leaders in particular, Sanballat the Horonite and Tobiah the Ammonite (people who had exercised some control in the land in the Israelites' absence), rose up against Nehemiah and his project. They did everything in their power to discourage Nehemiah, to cause him to abandon his task. They didn't want the Israelites to be reestablished in the land and regain their former power and glory.

Anytime you're halfway through a project, you are a prime candidate for discouragement. You're tired from what you've done and wondering if the end is actually attainable. When the people began to hear Tobiah's and Sanballat's words and warnings directed toward Nehemiah, they began to grow discouraged as well. What was Nehemiah to do? How did he defeat discouragement in his own life and keep hundreds and hundreds of his fellow Israelites from throwing up their hands in despair as well?

The lessons we will learn from the life of Nehemiah will keep us from giving in to the giant of discouragement. By the end of this lesson, you'll have learned from Nehemiah how to guard your own heart and mind. You'll have learned how to stay encouraged.

Recognizing Discouragement

Recognizing what makes us vulnerable to discouragement is the best way to keep it at a distance.

Discouragement Factor Number One: Fatigue

In verse 10 of Nehemiah 4, we learn that the "strength of the laborers [was] failing." Because we know the wall was finished in fifty-two days (Nehemiah 6:15), they must have been working non-stop for nearly a month when the opposition surfaced. Twenty-five or thirty days of hard work with little rest would have left the entire work force fatigued.

Someone has said that fatigue makes cowards of us all. I've seen it happen to me—perhaps you have as well. We are absolutely more vulnerable to discouragement when we are tired. I have had to acknowledge as I have gotten older that I simply can't push myself as hard as I once could. And when I try to, I quickly become unproductive. I've recognized that my basic personality type—do more, accomplish more—is probably not going to change at this point. But what I have learned to change is the way I work. When I'm working, I still work hard as we all should. But I've learned to take time to rest and recuperate. Instead of those breaks keeping me from accomplishing work, they actually enable me to do more in the long run. It's a matter of living life like a marathon instead of a sprint. As a result, I find I keep the giant of discouragement from interfering with accomplishing my goals.

Discouragement Factor Number Two: Frustration

Not only was the strength of the workers failing, but there was so much rubbish in the way from the prior wall's destruction that they could hardly work (verse 10).

You can imagine the scene—huge piles of stone blocks piled everywhere from when the Babylonians had knocked down the walls to capture the city. Sometimes laying the foundation for a project can be the most frustrating part. While it's perhaps the most important part, it's not nearly as much fun to clear the site and get ready to build as it is to see the walls rising. Moving the mountains of debris could easily have produced mountains of frustration.

There are three ways to live life: live out, wear out, or burn out. While I hope to live out, as you probably do too, some people think burning out is more spiritual. But it is not. People get burned out

because they work hard without focus, purpose, or accomplishment. I know people who work incredibly hard all the time, but they never burn out because they are reaching their goals and living with a tremendous sense of accomplishment. Burning out comes from trying to accomplish something that is unattainable or at least appears that way from where you stand. Trying to build a wall on top of piles of rubble could easily lead to burnout.

Burnout could be synonymous with frustration, and frustration is an early warning sign for the onset of discouragement. It's easy for people who are tired and frustrated to conclude they are going to fail.

Discouragement Factor Number Three: Failure

Finally in verse 10 we see the potential for failure that had set in: "We are not able to build the wall." It's easy to see why they would think they might fail, being exhausted and hemmed in by rubble on every side when they were just halfway done. You can imagine the workers beginning to talk among themselves as they worked, fueling the fires of failure with their discouraging and frustrating words.

Failure itself is a giant which all of us face at some point in our lives (we will devote an entire lesson to failure in our study). We have to remember that, in a fallen world, failure is part of life. Failing is not the issue, but what we do when we fail is. How we respond to failure, as well as how we respond to exhaustion and frustration, is what makes the difference regarding discouragement.

If, when we fail, we allow the final stepping stone to discouragement—fear—to be laid, we have made a way for this giant to walk right in.

Discouragement Factor Number Four: Fear

In verses 11 and 12, those working on the walls get word of their adversaries' plans: They mean to put the Jews to death. Those who opposed the rebuilding of the walls were coming in among the Israelites and whispering in their ears, "We're going to get you."

We shouldn't be surprised at that sort of tactic resulting in fear. Relentless criticism from one's enemies can begin to take its toll over time. Occasionally I receive a critical letter from someone who has heard me speak or read something I've written. It seems that those letters always arrive at the most inopportune time. You may be struggling already, and you open the mail and discover someone is out to get you (not literally, but with words). And you start believing

the criticism, wondering if you ought even to continue the work you're trying to accomplish. Criticism (threats in Nehemiah's case) can lead to fear, and fear can definitely lead to discouragement.

So . . . how do we respond when we are tired, frustrated, on the verge of failure, and fearful about the future? How do we keep from getting stuck in the slough of discouragement?

RESPONDING TO DISCOURAGEMENT

Let's follow the order of events in Nehemiah 4, to see how Nehemiah handled the pending possibility of serious discouragement.

Cry Out to God

The first thing he did, which is often the last thing we do, was to cry out to God (verses 4, 9). How often we find ourselves saying, "We've nothing left to do but pray." Instead of ending up praying, we ought to begin by praying.

The first place to begin when discouragement sets in is prayer, to ask God to intervene in the issues at hand. Often, when I am on the verge of discouragement, I will sit down at my computer or with my journal and write out my thoughts to the Lord as a prayer. Writing out my concerns helps me identify and crystallize the issues, helps me to focus and prioritize what has become a swirl of conflicting thoughts and feelings. But in the process of writing, I am also crying out to the Lord. That is always the place to begin.

Next, I turn to the Psalms of the Old Testament and encourage you to do so as well. We can think of the Psalms as the journal entries of David and the other psalmists. We get to peek into their journals and read their most intimate thoughts when they were going through times of discouragement. They become our mentors, our teachers, in learning how to cry out to God when we are discouraged.

Continue the Work God Has Given You to Do

Next, in verse 6, we find that they kept working in spite of the looming opposition. It is so easy to throw in the towel when we get discouraged. We want to rid ourselves of what we think is causing the frustration and discouragement. Ironically, by giving up we separate ourselves from the one thing that can help us overcome discouragement: achieving what we set out to do. When discouraging and accusing words came against Nehemiah, he continued doing exactly what he was doing before the attacks started! He didn't let the opposition keep him from accomplishing what he set out to do.

On one occasion Nehemiah's enemies tried to entice Nehemiah to come down off the wall and meet with them in a conference. I love Nehemiah's response. He replied to his enemies that he wasn't about to leave the great work he was doing and waste time meeting with them (Nehemiah 6:3)! What was he saying? He was sending a message of commitment and determination to finish what he knew God had called him to do.

The longer I live the more I realize that when I feel least like doing something, that is the time I most need to do it. Whether it's praying, exercising, resting, reading the Bible—whatever it is, there will always be times when we won't feel encouraged about the prospects of that activity being beneficial. But it will be. And we need to do it most at the time we feel least like doing it.

Concentrate on the Big Picture

In Nehemiah 4:13 and 14, Nehemiah rallies the workers to continue their work in light of a bigger picture. They weren't just stacking blocks, nor were they just building a little section of a wall. Rather, they were building a huge wall that would enclose the city of Jerusalem and protect them and their families from those seeking to do them harm.

Sometimes, working in our little corner of the Kingdom, it's easy to get discouraged. We wonder if what we're doing is making any difference or whether it's worth the trouble to continue on. Nehemiah's workers were in danger of isolation, not being able to see around the pile of rubble between them and the next group of workers further down the line. So Nehemiah positioned the workers so they could see better, could keep in touch with one another, and could remain encouraged in their work. Discouragement often comes when we lose sight of the big picture. We need to stay connected to a larger community of faith so we don't lose heart.

Leith Anderson, in his 1999 book *Leadership That Works*, helps Christian leaders in the same way. He cites page after page of highly encouraging facts and statistics about the progress of the Gospel around the world—and in America. Many people don't realize that, at that point, more people attended church in America each week than attended major sporting events in a year in our country. They also don't realize that there were nearly twice as many people in their twenties in church each Sunday than in their seventies. Numbers may be different now, but the Church is still making an impact today. That encourages us to stay focused on the big picture.

Claim the Encouragement of God's Promises

In verse 14 Nehemiah challenges the people to "not be afraid of [their enemies]. Remember the Lord, great and awesome." The promises of God are the bedrock of our faith. When we are toying with discouragement and entertaining things in our mind that are not true, we need nothing more than the truth from God. And His Word is where we go to find it. Take your Bible out, plant yourself in a chair, and start reading—out loud if necessary. Sometimes I will purpose before God to keep reading His Word until He comes and speaks to my heart in a way that helps me see through my discouragement. And He always does.

The Word of God tells us not to get discouraged in the midst of the good we are doing (Galatians 6:9). Taking an admonition like that to heart consistently is a powerful antidote to discouragement in life and ministry.

Carry Somebody Else's Burden

Finally, in Nehemiah 4:16-23 we find something very interesting taking place: people helping people. Some people were carrying, some were guarding, some were building—and all with swords strapped on. They even stayed up all night to continue the work (verses 22-23). What happens in that kind of environment? Teamwork, camaraderie, and community develop when we work together. The sharing of tasks keeps us dependent on one another. It's easier to do your part of a task than to try to do the whole thing by yourself. It's also much easier for synergy to occur, creating something "bigger than the sum of its parts" when everyone works together.

Many have been the times when I was lifted out of discouragement by getting involved in helping someone else. When I focus on others, I stop focusing on myself; and I discover in the process that others relieve their discouragement by reaching out to me. We reap what we sow (Galatians 6:7), and sowing encouragement into others' lives means we will reap it ourselves in time.

We live in potentially discouraging days. But arresting discouragement before it ever gets on the property of our heart and mind will keep it from taking over and stopping the work God is doing in and through us.

1. Turn to Nehemiah 4.

   a. What project did Nehemiah set out to accomplish in verse 6?

   b. What opposition did he and the Israelites face in verses 7-8?

   c. In time, what type of discouragement did the Israelites face according to verse 10?

   d. Like the Israelites, have you ever felt that your goals were unattainable? If so, did those goals lead to a burnout? Explain.

   e. What did the Israelites' adversaries plan to do against them? (verses 11-12)

   f. Rather than letting discouragement creep in, what is one way you can prevent it? (verses 4, 9) What ways do you currently handle discouragement?

g. How did Nehemiah respond to his enemies in Nehemiah 6:3?

h. In verses 13 and 14, how did Nehemiah encourage the Israelites? What was his purpose in doing so?

i. In verses 22-23, what took place among the community of Israelites? Why is it important to stay connected to community when working on a special project or goal?

2. Read Galatians 6:9.

   a. In spite of life's challenges, we are not to grow weary of what?

   b. In what season will we reap? But only if we do not lose what?

   c. How has this verse encouraged you to carry on in the work of the Lord?

1. Review Nehemiah 4 together.

   a. Discuss the opposition Nehemiah and the Israelites faced when rebuilding the wall in Jerusalem. (verses 1-8)

   b. How did they handle this form of opposition according to verse 9?

   c. What discouragement did they face in verse 10? Have you faced this type of discouragement in your own life? Discuss what you did to prevent this giant from interfering with accomplishing your goals.

   d. According to the lesson, what three options do we have for living life in the midst of frustration? What do you most often do? (See "Discouragement Factor Number Two: Frustration.")

   e. When we fail at a project or goal, what final stepping stone to discouragement do we need to prevent from being laid?

f. Why were the Israelites afraid in verses 11-12?

2. Discuss the five ways in which we are to respond to discouragement as the Israelites did, according to the following verses:

   a. Nehemiah 4:4, 9:

   b. Nehemiah 4:6:

   c. Nehemiah 4:13-14:

   d. Nehemiah 4:14; Galatians 6:9:

   e. Nehemiah 4:16-23:

3. According to Galatians 6:7, what happens when we help someone else in their time of need? Share ways you can sow into others' lives in your community.

DID YOU KNOW?

Nehemiah is both an interesting character and book of the Bible. Nehemiah was a royal cupbearer who was appointed governor of Jerusalem to oversee the restoration of that great city (and especially of its walls). As a prominent figure in the Bible, it is interesting to note that Nehemiah is never quoted in the New Testament. And historical evidence suggests that the books of Ezra and Nehemiah at one time may have been just one tome that was separated into two books at some later date.

SLAYING THE GIANT OF LONELINESS

Selected Scriptures

In this lesson we identify the pervasiveness of loneliness and map out a strategy for escaping its effects.

John Donne wrote, "No man is an island," yet Western nations have become gatherings of intimate strangers. In the midst of crowded cities and family rooms, loneliness afflicts many. While loneliness may sometimes be inevitable, its effects can be avoided.

I. **The Experience of Loneliness**
   A. The Lonely Single
   B. The Lonely Spouse
   C. The Lonely Survivor
   D. The Lonely Senior Citizen
   E. The Lonely Sufferer
   F. The Lonely Servant of God

II. **The Examples of Loneliness in the Bible**
   A. David the King
   B. Jeremiah the Prophet
   C. Paul the Apostle

III. **The Escape From Loneliness**
   A. Acknowledge the Reality of Your Loneliness
   B. Accept God's Provision for Your Loneliness
   C. Allow God's Word to Fill Your Mind and Heart
   D. Activate Your Network of Christian Friends

In his 1989 book *Six Hours One Friday*, author Max Lucado writes about taking a walk through an old cemetery in his hometown. Many of the graves were of people who lived and died in the nineteenth century. Many of the names belonged to children, bearing witness to the difficulties of life on the Texas prairie.

One grave he came across struck him sharply. It had no dates of birth or death, just the name of a woman and her two husbands. The epitaph on the grave read simply,

> Sleeps but rests not.
> Loved but was loved not.
> Tried to please, but pleased not.
> Died as she lived—alone.

What a sad testimony, to have lived and died alone. We tend to think life among the pioneers and settlers might have been more lonely than our lives. No telephones or dependable mail system, no neighbors close by to keep company with. But the truth is just the opposite. Loneliness has reached epidemic proportions in our modern world. Even though we have multiple ways at our fingertips to communicate with the outside world, people today are lonelier than they have ever been in history.

Because loneliness creates a feeling of emptiness on the inside, people try to compensate for that feeling by filling themselves with food, drugs, alcohol, material things, sex, work, or other people's lives. Loneliness is not removed by substitutes for true relationships in life—the most foundational being our relationship with God. Everyone experiences loneliness at different times in life, and it is not always a bad or dangerous experience. There is something to be said for learning to be alone with ourselves and God. But loneliness over the long term can have negative effects physically as well as spiritually.

In this lesson we'll talk about the experience of loneliness in life, study some characters in Scripture who experienced loneliness, and learn how to escape the negative effects of loneliness.

THE EXPERIENCE OF LONELINESS

Different stages of our lives result in different kinds of loneliness. As you read through this lesson, you'll no doubt identify with one or more of these significant times of loneliness.

The Lonely Single

The extended community in which I reside, San Diego, California, has one of the largest single populations in the United States. Whether it's for the beautiful weather, the California lifestyle, the many entrepreneurial ventures, or the military bases, young single adults flock to San Diego. I know from my own relationships with single Christians that going home to an empty house or apartment night after night can

be a lonely lifestyle. And this is true not only in my community, but everywhere. The burgeoning singles' bar and club scene in America is just one indication of how desperate many single people are to conquer loneliness by meeting someone—anyone—to talk to. Being a Christian helps—a single believer in Christ has spiritual resources to draw on in times of loneliness. But human beings were not created by God to spend their life alone (Genesis 2:18). And by that I don't mean marriage exclusively—but in the presence of other people.

The Lonely Spouse

It is an amazement to me that the institution God created to provide the greatest sense of intimacy often becomes a place of great loneliness. I remember speaking somewhere on this topic and receiving a letter in the mail the next week from a woman who had heard my message. She wrote, "Today you really struck a spot that is sensitive in my heart. I try not to dwell on it—the loneliness in marriage, but the truth is I am lonely. My husband and I are both Christians. We live relatively well. We are educated, and my husband is a good man. He works hard and is a good provider. He isn't abusive, and he is a fairly good father. But my emotional needs are very rarely met because he works all the time. It's the case of two people living parallel lives but never really meeting at all. He has heard and read a little about how a husband can create a good relationship with his wife, but it must all pass over him without making an impression. . . . I try not to think about it. But the hurt is deep. I am a very lonely person."

It is sad that the very relationship God ordained to combat loneliness has become for many the most lonely place on earth.

The Lonely Survivor

Then there are the lonely survivors, the spouses who live on after a loved one has died. Lonely survivors experience a kind of pain which, I am told, is so intense that there is nothing in life to which it can be compared. Not having gone through that loss personally, I can only imagine what it must be like. While the death of a spouse is heart-rending, at least it comes with a sense of closure. Divorce is another kind of loneliness-producer that is perhaps even worse, for there is no finality. It is an open wound that rarely heals completely. Not only is there physical and emotional loneliness to contend with but a sense of rejection as well.

The Lonely Senior Citizen

The number of senior citizens in our country is growing at a faster rate than at any time in history. The sense of loneliness that sets in with seniors is significant. Often they have lost a spouse, their children have moved away, and they struggle to find a place to fit in where they can feel significant. The position of authority, influence, and respect they occupied in their vocational years is no longer theirs, and so their loneliness is one of significance as much as personal contact. For today's

seniors, the sense of loneliness that comes from a loss of significance is often the most acute kind of loneliness there is. Searching for, and finding, a purpose in the twilight years of life is a great challenge.

The Lonely Sufferer

There is the lonely sufferer who experiences the pain he cannot describe to anyone else. Sometimes that loneliness is in a busy place like a hospital. One man wrote to me from his hospital bed: "It is when the lights go out and the room is suddenly plunged into darkness that the awful awareness comes. The traffic of the hospital goes on like an uncontrolled fever outside my door. But inside, the room is so still." Loneliness can be compounded by suffering. Many suffer physically or emotionally in ways that cannot be described or be cured instantly. The loneliness Job felt was not just because he had lost his family but because he was suffering physically in the midst of his loss.

The Lonely Servant of God

What can I say about the person who leaves his familiar culture and goes to the mission field, leaving behind everything and everyone that kept him from being lonely? He goes into a brand new culture where everything is different—food, language, customs—and he doesn't know anyone on a personal level. It takes far more time to establish new relationships because of the cultural barriers which must be overcome. We get letters from missionaries in which you can read tales of loneliness written between the lines. They are not complaining — but you can tell they are paying a price for their service to God on a foreign mission field.

Leadership can be a lonely place. Moses said, "I cannot carry all these people by myself; the burden is too heavy for me" (Numbers 11:14, NIV). Anyone who has ever been in a position of leadership knows that it can be lonely "at the top." When a leader moves out ahead of those he is leading, he is turning his back on those who follow. You can be the leader of a large church or a large ministry organization and still experience loneliness. It comes with the territory.

We can find great heroes of the faith in Scripture who experienced loneliness in their lives. It is not a sin to be lonely, for great men and women of God have battled loneliness. We can develop a sinful response to loneliness, but it is not a sin to experience those feelings from time to time. Seeing that others have been lonely can make us know that we are not alone in our feelings.

THE EXAMPLES OF LONELINESS IN THE BIBLE

David the King

David wrote on one occasion, "For my days are consumed like smoke, and my bones are burned like a hearth. . . . I am like a pelican of

the wilderness; I am like an owl of the desert. I lie awake, and am like a sparrow alone on the housetop" (Psalm 102:3, 6-7). You can almost feel the edge of David's pain as he describes his feelings. David was hounded all over the Judean wilderness by King Saul as a fugitive for much of his pre-royal life. When I read about David's loneliness, it comforts and instructs me to know that he survived and trusted God in the midst of it.

Jeremiah the Prophet

The story of Jeremiah the prophet is one of the most agonizing stories you will ever read. Jeremiah was also the author of the book of Lamentations, a collection of funeral dirges expressing the anguish of his heart as he watched the city of Jerusalem go down in ruin before his very eyes. Jeremiah is known as the weeping prophet because of the tears he shed over the destruction of God's city. No one would listen to his calls for repentance whereby the city might be saved. He was a lonely voice crying out in a spiritual wilderness. He finally confessed that he would be better off leaving and going out into the desert than remaining among those who cared so little for God (Jeremiah 9:2). For him, the loneliness of the wilderness would have been better than the loneliness he felt among his own people.

Paul the Apostle

Paul wrote most of the New Testament, founded missionary churches all over the Mediterranean world, and penned the greatest theological treatise of all time in the letter to the Romans. Would someone like Paul suffer from loneliness? On occasion he did.

At the end of the last letter he wrote before he died, addressed to his protégé Timothy, he found himself in a Roman prison. This was not the setting of his first arrest in Rome which was more like a house-arrest (Acts 28:30). This time, he was imprisoned in a Roman dungeon. Listen to the words he wrote to Timothy which give evidence of his loneliness: "Be diligent to come to me quickly; for Demas has forsaken me, having loved this present world, and has departed for Thessalonica—Crescens for Galatia, Titus for Dalmatia. Only Luke is with me. . . . And Tychicus I have sent to Ephesus. . . . Alexander the coppersmith did me much harm. . . . At my first defense no one stood with me, but all forsook me. May it not be charged against them" (2 Timothy 4:9-16).

Do you feel that? Here is the great apostle, standing alone at the end of his life. No one is with him. You would think that could not happen after all he had done for the Church, but it did. We sense no resentment in Paul's words, only the fact of his aloneness.

When loneliness sweeps over you like a wave, remember you are not the first person to have been lonely, and not the first Christian. As I have said, it is no sin to be lonely. But it can become a sin if we indulge it and allow it to turn to self-pity. God has given us ways to escape from loneliness before it becomes a downward spiral that pulls us down with it.

THE ESCAPE FROM LONELINESS

Here are four ways to defend yourself from the power of loneliness:

Acknowledge the Reality of Your Loneliness

Christians have made an art of denying the reality of some parts of life. Because it seems unspiritual to confess to being lonely, many Christians will quote Hebrews 13:5, where Christ said, "I will never leave you nor forsake you," and profess they are never lonely because He is always with them. Theologically it is true that Christ is always with the believer, but our practice doesn't always match our position. It is more honest, transparent, and real to simply say, "Yes, I am lonely at this time of my life," than to deny the reality of our situation. Human beings experience loneliness at times, and there is no shame in a Christian admitting that fact.

Accept God's Provision for Your Loneliness

Ultimately, God's provision for loneliness is the only suitable solution. There is a fundamental emptiness in every human being which can only be filled by the presence of God Himself. It is interesting to note that the only time Jesus Christ cried out in loneliness was from the cross when the Father forsook Him and allowed Him to die as a sacrifice for the world. Without the presence of God, the most agonizing loneliness will afflict even the strongest person. No person should search for a solution for his loneliness without solving the basic issue of separation from God. Accepting Jesus Christ, and being filled by His Spirit, is the first step toward overcoming the negative dimensions of loneliness.

Allow God's Word to Fill Your Mind and Heart

I say this so frequently that it can be misinterpreted as a Christian platitude. But it is not. I say it often because it is the absolute truth! Second only to the presence of God's Spirit in one's life is the presence of God's Word as an antidote to loneliness. God has spoken clearly; and if you read His Word, you will hear His voice.

Activate Your Network of Christian Friends

Let me close with a strong word, strong because it is true: Living in the house of loneliness is a choice. You may not have become lonely by choice, but remaining lonely is something you don't have to do. The Body of Christ exists to encourage and strengthen Christians; but if we refuse to get involved, it is difficult for that to happen. Each believer must assume the responsibility for his own emotional and spiritual health, including not lingering in loneliness. In the average church there are numerous "doors" through which one can enter into relationships of service and friendship. But you must walk through the door.

When we have Jesus Christ living in us, though the world may crumble around us, He is the light from on high that thrills and encourages our hearts. Look beyond your circumstances into the face of the One who loves you.

1. Read Genesis 2:18.

   a. Verse 18 says that it is not good for man to be what? Who said this?

   b. What does it signify if God declares that man should not be alone?

   c. What is God's response to this situation? (verse 18)

   d. Why do you think loneliness sometimes exists within the confines of marriage?

2. Can you or someone you know identify with the lonely survivor or lonely senior citizen? What are some ways you or those you know currently combat that loneliness?

3. Read Numbers 11:14.

   a. How did Moses react to his position of leadership?

b. Have you ever led a group of people or gone to the mission field and felt a sense of loneliness? How did you continue on in your work?

4. Describe David's, Jeremiah's, and Paul's experiences with loneliness according to the following verses.

   a. Psalm 102:3, 6-7

   b. Jeremiah 9:2

   c. 2 Timothy 4:9-16

5. What confidence do we have in Christ when it comes to loneliness? (Hebrews 13:5)

   a. How much time do you spend in God's Word each week?

   b. Whom do you spend time with? Are you involved in your church?

   c. Why do you think these habits are crucial in combating loneliness?

1. Review the different stages of loneliness as mentioned in the lesson.

   a. According to Genesis 2:18, what is God's intention for mankind? What types of relationships does this refer to?

   b. Are there any lonely survivors in your group? How can the group best comfort them today?

   c. Why do many seniors suffer from loneliness? Besides the loss of a spouse or having family far away, what have they often lost their sense of?

   d. If you know any lonely sufferers today, how can you as a group best reach out to them?

   e. Is loneliness a sin? Discuss why or why not.

2. Heroes of the faith suffered from loneliness in their lives, just as we sometimes do today.

   a. What did King David compare himself to in Psalm 102:3, 6-7?

b. What did Jeremiah confess in Jeremiah 9:2?

c. Though Paul the apostle did much for the Church, what do we discover about him in 2 Timothy 4:9-16?

3. Discuss the ways in which we can defend ourselves from the power of loneliness.

a. Review Hebrews 13:5 and recall the ways this verse has played out in your own life.

b. If you are struggling with loneliness today, discuss it with the group if comfortable. Pray for those who are struggling today.

DID YOU KNOW?

You can use those lonely times in your life to cry out to God and strengthen and deepen your relationship with Him. Multiple times in Scripture we find Jesus praying by Himself. In His greatest moment of loneliness and agony, we find Jesus praying to His Father in the Garden of Gethsemane, where the disciples nearby were no comfort or company to Him (Matthew 26:36-40). And many forget that before Jesus walked on the water to the disciples, He was completely alone, once again in prayer to His Father on the mountain (Matthew 14:22-25).

SLAYING THE GIANT OF WORRY

Matthew 6:25-34

*In this lesson we learn why worry is a fruitless exercise
—a waste of one's time.*

OUTLINE

Years ago a popular song contained the now-famous lyric, "Don't worry, be happy!" That's not bad advice, but it's incomplete: We need a reason not to worry in order to be happy. There are two reasons: Worry is fruitless, and God is in control of everything.

I. **Facing the Giant of Worry**
    A. Worry Is Inconsistent
    B. Worry Is Irrational
    C. Worry Is Ineffective
    D. Worry Is Illogical
    E. Worry Is Irreligious

II. **Fighting the Giant of Worry**
    A. To Win Over Worry, We Need a System of Priorities
    B. To Win Over Worry, We Need a Strategic Program

At the very moment you are reading the words on this page, you are probably (if you're like most people) worried about something! Let's face it—everyone encounters the huge giant of worry at times. And that's where we've arrived in our study of the giants we meet in our spiritual experience.

Corrie ten Boom used to say, "Worry is an old man with bended head, carrying a load of feathers which he thinks are lead." That's a beautiful, non-technical definition of *worry*—being anxious about something that doesn't exist in fact but which we believe does or might exist. The New Testament word for *worry* is translated by the phrase "to take thought" or "to be careful." It comes from a Greek word which means "to have a divided mind." So, to be a worrier is to have your mind divided between legitimate thoughts and thoughts that are not legitimate, thoughts which you shouldn't be thinking.

Worry is future-focused. The person who worries has two problems: The future is not here, and the future is not his. Worrying cannot change the future nor can it control the future. Jesus said it was wrong to worry. In His words in Matthew 6:25-34 (our text for this lesson), three times He said, "Do not worry." Those words give us our marching orders for defeating the giant of worry.

Before we study Jesus' words, let me tell you what "Do not worry" doesn't mean. First, it doesn't mean "Don't plan." The King James Version of Matthew 6:34 says, "Take therefore no thought for the morrow." That almost sounds like, "Don't think about tomorrow," which is not what it means. Jesus Himself certainly planned, and the Scriptures support the idea of being responsible in our approach to the future. Not worrying is not the same as not planning.

Second, Jesus is not saying, "Don't ever be concerned." We are not to float through life on a breeze of indifference, ignoring the realities around us. There are plenty of things in life to be morally, spiritually, and practically concerned about as a Christian. But not worrying is not the same thing as not being concerned.

So, when Jesus says, "Do not worry," He doesn't mean "Don't plan" and He doesn't mean "Don't be concerned." He means don't get so exercised about the things which you have no control that you paralyze yourself and those who depend on you. Worry and anxiety change nothing except the worrier—and it's always in negative ways.

FACING THE GIANT OF WORRY

We will divide Jesus' words about worry into two sections. In verses 25-32 we will discover why worry is a fruitless endeavor.

Worry Is Inconsistent

It doesn't make sense to conclude that God has already done the biggest job (creating our body, our life) but then would fail to do the smaller job (providing what we need to live the life He has given us). It is an argument from the greater to the lesser. God obviously knew what it would take for bodies like ours to exist—food, clothing, and shelter (verse 25). It is completely inconsistent with the wise and loving character of God to think that He did the one thing without also doing the other. When we worry about our future provision of food, clothing, and shelter, we actually malign the character of our God. Our bodies, our very lives, are clear evidence that God is a creator and provider. For Him not to feed, clothe, and shelter that which He has created doesn't make sense.

Worry Is Irrational

Verse 26 shows how irrational worry is. Verse 25 dealt with the question of whether God is able to provide. The answer is "Yes" since He has already done the harder job of creating life. Now Jesus takes up the question: "Will He provide?" Whereas He argued from the greater to the lesser in verse 25, here He speaks from the lesser to the greater: "If God provides for something as simple as the birds of the air, won't He also provide for you?" It's irrational to think that He wouldn't.

In Matthew 10:29-31 Jesus says that two sparrows can be bought for a copper coin, and Luke 12:6 says that five sparrows can be bought for two coins. So it appears that the market for sparrows was like this: Buy two for a penny, but if you buy four, they throw in a fifth sparrow for free. Jesus is saying that not even the most inexpensive and smallest parts of God's creation change their status without it being part of His will (not even the hairs on our head—Matthew 10:30). Therefore, if tiny things like sparrows and hair are under His watchful eye and concern, how much more are we who are the pinnacle of His creation. Will He care for us? The answer is: "Of course He will!"

Worry Is Ineffective

Not only is worry inconsistent and irrational, it is also ineffective. Verse 27 asks, "How can worrying add anything to your life?" Answer: It can't. Worry is totally ineffective when it comes to improving or changing your prospects for the future.

Jesus uses the cubit as an illustration to make His point. A cubit was the standard unit of measure in biblical days, equal to about eighteen inches in length. Jesus asks, in essence, "How many of you can sit there in a chair and worry all day about your height and add eighteen inches to it?" The answer is, again, no one. You could worry all day and not change one thing about yourself—except make your hair a bit more gray!

It's likely that Jesus meant something deeper than just the issue of height. It's possible that He was referring to the length of one's life: Who, by worrying, can add any length to his life? And, of course, the answer is no one. In fact, the opposite is probably true. Cemeteries are no doubt filled with people whose lives were shortened by worry. Doctors are discovering more and more negative effects of worry, stress, anger, and anxiety on the human body. Instead of lengthening your life, worry might shorten it. Worry doesn't change tomorrow, but it sure changes today. Worry robs you of the strength and ability to enjoy the gift of life today that God wants you to enjoy.

Worry Is Illogical

The fourth truth about worry is that it is illogical. Jesus next turns to nature, the beautiful lilies of the field which God has clothed in glorious splendor—and does so year after year. We know far more about the beauty of nature today than was apparent in biblical days. We have discovered unbelievable beauty in the flora and fauna of this earth which are even more astounding than lilies. Therefore, the point Jesus makes here should be even more obvious to us today than it was to His disciples.

Solomon was the richest, and therefore the most beautifully-dressed, sovereign in the world. Yet even Solomon's golden glory could not compare with the delicate beauty of the flowers of the field who are clothed effortlessly by God every spring. Is it logical to think that God, who clothes the flowers in splendor, will not also clothe those whom He has created? No, it is completely illogical (verses 28-30).

Jesus' argument is based on nature, that which God Himself took the initiative to create and "clothe." If mankind is the pinnacle of creation (Psalm 8), we should expect that God would assume the responsibility for providing for our clothing as well.

Worry Is Irreligious

The final fault to be found with worry is that it betrays our spiritual heritage. In verses 31 and 32, Jesus compares those within

Israel who worry about the future to the Gentiles. This is not to be a put-down of non-Jewish people. Rather it is a statement about religious heritage. Gentiles were the pagans or heathens of the world who were either idolaters or atheists. They either worshiped wood and stone idols or no god at all. In that case, they had every right to be worried about the future.

But for those who claim to have a personal relationship with the Creator God of heaven and earth, worrying is a complete contradiction of what we say we believe. To worry is to act like there is no God who has promised to take care of us. That doesn't mean Christians don't have momentary worries. Ask any parent who has raised teenagers, and you'll discover that worries are a consistent part of life. But the key is to take a momentary worry and use it as a springboard to a mature, spiritual response. Meeting worry is inevitable; moving in with worry is not. When we make worry our constant companion, we betray our spiritual heritage.

But Jesus doesn't rebuke us. Notice how tenderly He concludes this section: "Your heavenly Father knows that you need all these things." Jesus knows that worry is a liability of living in this fallen world. But He wants us to learn that worry is a leaky boat, incapable of transporting us safely to the shore of the future. There is a safer way to get there—defeat the giant of worry by seeking God's Kingdom and righteousness above all.

Fighting the Giant of Worry

To defeat the giant of worry, two things are needed: priorities for today and a plan for compartmentalizing yesterday and tomorrow.

To Win Over Worry, We Need a System of Priorities

Much of the worry that destroys people is the worry of a divided heart. A divided heart cannot decide what it believes and therefore how it is going to live. It gets caught up in every wind of change that blows through society. A person without priorities will constantly find his heart captured by (and worried about) everything that "might" be.

Jesus said to focus in on only one thing in life: the Kingdom of God and the values which it stands for (verse 33). When we do that, everything else in life will fall into place according to the will of God and according to His provision. The King takes care of those who dwell in His Kingdom.

Many Christians who worry do so because they know they have violated the priority of seeking God first. Not only do they worry about the future, they worry about worrying about the future! Worry becomes a cycle they cannot break. The only way to stop it is to jump off the merry-go-round of worry and ask, "What is the most important thing to me?" If you conclude that God is most important, you are ready to make a clean break with worry. Making God your priority will prepare you for developing a strategy for dealing with the yesterdays and tomorrows you used to worry about.

To Win Over Worry, We Need a Strategic Program

The final verse in this section holds what may be the key truth in understanding how to defeat the giant of worry: focus on today. No one ever sank under the burdens of today; but add yesterday and tomorrow to today, and it can capsize your life. Jesus said, "Sufficient for the day is its own trouble" (verse 34).

Dr. Osler, a famous physician of years past, made a helpful observation. He noted how ocean-going vessels were able to seal off various sections of the boat so that a leak could be contained in only one part of the ship. Though damaged, a ship could still make it to safety. Just so, he suggested, we need to develop the capacity for sealing off the yesterdays and tomorrows that fuel the fires of worry. We need to learn to live in the compartment of today alone.

1. Do Not Dwell on Your Tomorrows

What Jesus teaches in verse 34 probably has its roots in Deuteronomy 33:25: "As your days, so shall your strength be." That is, you will have strength from God as the events of your days require. As a pastor, I have counseled with many families through the years who have gone through devastating financial losses. When they express concerns about their future, I can only remind them of these truths. God promises to take care of today, and we are to trust Him for that.

We need to seal off the door that keeps us from worrying about tomorrow so that tomorrow doesn't sap today of its strength and vitality. But we also need to seal off our yesterdays—those days which are already in the history books and cannot be changed.

2. Do Not Dwell on Your Yesterdays

There are three things I have discovered people worrying about when it comes to yesterday: sins, successes, and sorrows—all unchangeable.

(a) We Worry About Yesterday's Sins

People who come to Christ out of a background stained by sin and wantonness often have a difficult time putting the memories of those things out of their minds. It is my privilege to remind such people, and all who have sinned, that God has put our sins as far from us as the east is from the west (Psalm 103:12). Or, if people agree that God has forgiven them, they say they cannot forgive themselves. In both cases, we need to allow God to seal us off from the sins of our past. The guilt and shame of them cannot leak into the compartment of today.

(b) We Worry About Yesterday's Successes

Sometimes those who have no problem sealing off their sin don't do as well sealing off their successes. Many who come into the Christian life having reached the pinnacle of success in their vocational career have a hard time switching priorities and focus. The apostle Paul was a young Jewish scholar on the fast track to success in Pharisaism when he met Christ. He closed the door on his past successes—"forgetting those things which are behind" (Philippians 3:13) —in order to focus on Christ and His Kingdom. We must learn to do the same.

(c) We Worry About Yesterday's Sorrows

This may be the hardest. We put aside sin and success, but the sorrow that lingers after life's tragedies and heartaches is often difficult to seal off. It's like sealing off a part of our own heart and soul, the place where sorrow lives. But we must learn to live in the present. God is the great "I AM" (Exodus 3:14), not "I WAS" or "I WILL BE." The Christian who lives with Him today, in the present tense, is the one who will be free from worries about yesterday, today, or tomorrow.

God will help you deal with the problems of today if you will follow His instructions about worry and "be anxious for nothing, but in everything by prayer and supplication, with thanksgiving, let your requests be made known to God; and the peace of God . . . will guard your hearts and minds through Christ Jesus" (Philippians 4:6-7).

The seven most important words for would-be worriers are: DON'T WORRY ABOUT ANYTHING—PRAY ABOUT EVERYTHING. You can face the giant of worry, and you can win.

PERSONAL QUESTIONS

1. Read Matthew 6:25-34.

   a. How many times is the phrase "Do not worry" repeated in this passage? Why do you think that phrase was reiterated multiple times?

   b. Does "Do not worry" mean we shouldn't be concerned about the cares of life? Why or why not?

   c. According to verse 25, what should we not worry about? What reason do we have for not worrying? (verse 26)

   d. What in your life has caused you to worry lately? Do you feel as if God provided for you in that instance?

   e. In verse 27, what question does Jesus ask? Why is that a good reason to stop worrying?

f. Why is worrying about what we wear illogical according to verses 28-30?

g. Whom, if we worry, are we compared to in verses 31-32? What reason do we have not to worry?

h. What are our instructions in verse 33? What will happen when we follow these instructions?

i. What day are we supposed to focus on? Why is worrying about the future a pointless and dangerous act? (See verse 34.)

j. Why should Christ-followers not worry about their past sins according to Psalm 103:12?

2. Is there something you're worried about from your past that is keeping you from living for God in the present?

1. Turn to Matthew 6:25-34.

   a. Discuss the difference between being concerned and being worried.

   b. Though God created our bodies, why is it that we still worry about everyday provisions like food and clothing?

   c. What do Matthew 10:29-31 and Luke 12:6 say about the sparrows? Yet how does God provide for them? (Matthew 6:26)

   d. What does worrying not do for our life? (verse 27)

   e. Discuss Psalm 8. Since mankind is the pinnacle of creation, what does that mean for us when it comes to worrying?

f. What are we betraying when we make worry our constant companion?

g. Discuss how worry can cause us to falter between living for God and living for the world. What are we to seek first? (verse 33)

h. Because today has enough trouble of its own, how should we handle the cares of yesterday and tomorrow? (verse 34; Philippians 3:13)

i. What does God provide for us each new day? (Deuteronomy 33:25)

j. What are God's instructions to us in Philippians 4:6-7? What will guard our hearts and minds?

2. Share about something that is worrying you lately. Is it something that already happened or has yet to happen? How can you encourage each other throughout the week to live in the present?

It is easy in retrospect to laugh at the worry and anxiety we carried for things that never happened. Do you remember that it was a matter of *when* and not *if* a nuclear war between the United States and the Soviet Union would break out? Or do you recall how the Y2K computer bug was going to send us into the dark ages at the turn of the millennium? While it is always good to prepare, a lot of needless anxiety and worry can be wasted on things we can't control. Instead, we need to adopt the attitude of James 4:15: "If the Lord wills, we shall live and do this or that."

SLAYING THE GIANT OF GUILT

Psalms 32 and 51

*In this lesson we learn the cause of guilt
and how to remove it.*

OUTLINE

Guilt has been called the gift that keeps on giving: It continues to remind us that we have sinned. Therefore guilt is a good thing—a motivator to help us regain a clear conscience. If we follow God's directives, we can be free of guilt and the stain of sin.

I. **The Agony of Guilt**
   A. Silence
   B. Sorrow
   C. Secrecy

II. **The Accusation of Guilt**

III. **The Admission of Guilt**
   A. He Accepts Full Responsibility for His Sin
   B. He Acknowledges the Sinfulness of Sin
   C. He Addresses His Confession to God

IV. **The Answer to Guilt**
   A. Removing the Sin
   B. Restoring the Joy
   C. Renewing the Fellowship
   D. Refocus on the Future

Many people don't know that King David of Israel battled two giants in his lifetime. Goliath is the well-known giant he defeated in a matter of minutes, but guilt is the lesser-known giant it took him many months to defeat.

David met the giant of guilt when he saw a beautiful woman from the roof of his palace and had her brought to him. He committed adultery with her and then sent her home. What he thought was going to be a simple and brief encounter became complicated when the woman, Bathsheba, sent him word that she was pregnant by him.

David felt he had to cover his sin or risk losing his reputation as a godly king. He sent for Bathsheba's husband, Uriah, who was away fighting in David's army. He figured Uriah would come home and have relations with Bathsheba, and it would then appear her pregnancy was caused by her husband, not David. But David did not plan on Uriah's loyalty and honor. Uriah refused to enjoy the comfort of his wife when his fellow soldiers were still in battle, so he spent the night outside David's palace.

When David realized his plan hadn't worked, he implemented a second plan—to have his army commander send Uriah into the heat of battle so he would be killed. And that is exactly what happened. David was then guilty of murder as well as adultery. Nine months later a child was born to Bathsheba. Through his own writings, we are introduced to David's state of mind and his actions following the birth of his child.

Two Psalms—Psalms 32 and 51—give us insight into what it was like for David to live with the guilt of his sin (Psalm 32) and the confession of his sin to God (Psalm 51). Defeating guilt, the giant of his philandering, became a far greater challenge than defeating Goliath, the giant of the Philistines.

THE AGONY OF GUILT

Psalm 32 describes in part the anguish of body and soul that David went through while concealing his sin.

Silence

David couldn't talk to the Lord about his sin, and therefore he couldn't talk to the Lord about anything. The Bible says, "If I regard iniquity in my heart, the Lord will not hear" (Psalm 66:18). So David no longer had fellowship with God. His heart became silent. His

communication with God was cut off. His guilt began to take on physiological dimensions. He said that his bones grew old through his groaning all the day long (verse 3). He apparently became physically incapacitated from carrying the guilt of what he had done.

Sorrow

He said, "For day and night Your hand was heavy upon me; my vitality was turned into the drought of summer" (verse 4). King David was still commanding all of his subjects as the king, but he could not command his own conscience. He was filled with agony. His freshness of life was gone, replaced with bitterness and anguish. His conscience was filled with disgust, breaking his communion with God. His life was a mess.

Secrecy

One reason he suffered so much was there was no one to whom he could convey his pain. Nobody knew what David had done except Bathsheba and Joab—and each of them only knew the half of it. His sin with Bathsheba may not have been planned, but his sin against Uriah was planned and premeditated. For over a year David tried to live with his secret guilt. He couldn't talk to God. He couldn't talk to his friends. He could only talk to himself, but he kept getting only condemnation from his own conscience. Guilt was wearing him away.

Then the Lord sent someone to help David with his problem—which brings us to the accusation of guilt.

THE ACCUSATION OF GUILT

God sent a prophet named Nathan to confront David about his sin. The Lord apparently revealed to Nathan what he needed to know about David's sin, and Nathan decided to use a story to call David to account (2 Samuel 12:1-7). It was a story of two men, one rich and one poor. When a traveler came by and needed some food, the rich man, instead of taking food from his own flocks, took the poor man's sole lamb and gave it to the traveler.

In this story, David is obviously the rich man, Uriah the poor man, and Bathsheba the lamb taken by the rich man. David has no idea Nathan is telling a story about him. He thinks this is something that actually happened in his kingdom, and he exclaimed, "The man who has done this shall surely die! . . . because he had no pity" (2 Samuel 12:5-6). Nathan then lowered the boom on David: "You are the man!" (verse 7)

It's hard to imagine a moment filled with more anguish and relief at the same time. While David was humiliated and ashamed, finally the secret sins he had carried for so many months were out in the open. It was now time for him to admit his guilt and move toward cleansing.

THE ADMISSION OF GUILT

We now move to Psalm 51, which says in its superscription (at the beginning of the Psalm), "A Psalm of David when Nathan the prophet went to him, after he had gone in to Bathsheba." What we have in Psalm 51 is David's response to his confrontation with Nathan the prophet. In this Psalm we discover the pattern for defeating the giant of guilt in our own lives.

He Accepts Full Responsibility for His Sin

Step one in defeating guilt is accepting full responsibility for sin. You might take a colored highlighter pen and go down through Psalm 51 and highlight each first person singular pronoun: I, me, my. You'll get a good indication of exactly how precise David was in his confession. He was not avoiding the fact that he was the one who had sinned and was guilty before God.

Taking responsibility for sin is almost a lost art in our day and time. We have learned to excuse and rationalize almost every conceivable act. But guilt is only removed when it is acknowledged and confessed. Sin is like a stain on a table top. You may hide it by putting a plate over it, but the stain is still there. It only comes off by removing what's hiding it and dealing with the stain itself. That's what David did.

He Acknowledges the Sinfulness of Sin

In three verses David uses four different words to describe what he has done: transgression, iniquity, sin, and evil (verses 1-2, 4). Each of these words expresses a different aspect of breaking God's law. When we confess our sin we are saying the same thing about it that God says about it. If we don't say the same thing God says, we haven't confessed. In Psalm 32:5 David said, "I acknowledged my sin to You, and my iniquity I have not hidden. I said, 'I will confess my transgressions to the Lord.'" That's saying it like it is.

Even in America, there was a day when people were scared of sin. They fled from it and hated it and feared that concealing it might threaten their very salvation. But today we find people using every word except "sin" to describe behavior that is offensive to God.

When it comes to our sin, we mumble instead of confess. We find teachers asking rebellious children how it made them feel when they stole another child's lunch money. We find the word "sin" appearing on dessert menus, describing the decadence of chocolate fudge. We have so insulated ourselves against the concept of sin that our modern generation thinks nothing of living with all kinds of sins unconfessed in their lives. And the Church is in danger of adopting that mentality as well. We don't need to model David's sin, but we do need to model his confession.

He Addresses His Confession to God

Notice that he says it is ultimately against God that he has sinned (verse 4). It's not that David was insensitive to the reality of the damage he had brought to other people's lives. He is saying that he realizes sin is first and foremost a violation of God's holy standards and that God is the one before whom confession and repentance is due. If we go and ask another person to forgive us before we have confessed our sin to God, then we have misunderstood the priorities of confession. Of course we should ask forgiveness of the people our sin has hurt. But above all, a holy God is most offended by our sin and to Him our confession should first go.

THE ANSWER TO GUILT

There are three steps to the complete removal of sin in the sight of God and man: Remove the sin, restore the joy, and renew the fellowship (51:7-12).

Removing the Sin

If the confession of sin is the bad news, then the removal of it is the good news. And David addresses sin's removal with a variety of language equal to that which he used to describe his sin: "Wash me thoroughly . . . cleanse me . . . . Purge me . . . wash me . . . . blot out" (verses 2, 7, 9). As mentioned before, sin is like a stain. The word "cleanse" was also used to refer to the cleansing of a leper in the Old Testament. It is as if David is saying, "Cleanse the leprosy-like sin which has afflicted my soul."

When a person in Old Testament Israel came into contact with a dead body, he had to be ceremonially cleansed with hyssop. Here David says, "Purge me with hyssop," probably a reference to the death of Uriah which he caused. "Blot out all my iniquities" probably refers to the fact that there was no sacrifice for murder and adultery in the Old Testament. David asks for mercy, that God would blot the sins out of His book.

Once the sins are blotted out, the joy which the sins took away needs to be restored. That is David's next request.

Restoring the Joy

In verses 8 and 12 David prays that God will return to him the joy of salvation he enjoyed before. David isn't asking for God to restore his salvation, but the joy of his salvation. David's salvation wasn't lost when he sinned, nor is ours. What was lost was the joy and refreshment of soul which salvation brings, which definitely will be lost when we try to hide our sin from God. We can think of the time David danced for sheer joy before the Lord as the ark of the covenant was transported up to Mount Zion in Jerusalem (2 Samuel 6:14). We do not get the impression from Scripture that David was a moody, downcast individual. From the many songs (psalms) he wrote and the enthusiasm with which he lived life, we can suspect that he took great joy in his relationship with God. But that joy had disappeared like the morning mist as a result of his concealed sin. And now he wants that joy back. He is tired of having his vitality drained daily like pond water in a time of drought. He wants to be filled afresh with the joy of salvation.

You probably know the feeling David had. No matter what the sin, joy is lost when sin is not confessed. A Christian with unconfessed sin in his life will be far more miserable than a non-Christian. Why? Because the Christian knows what the joy of the Lord is like and knows what he is missing by not being in fellowship with God. A person who has never experienced the joy of salvation could not know what that is like.

When the joy of salvation is restored, fellowship can be renewed —both with God and with man.

Renewing the Fellowship

When David prays not to be cast away from God's presence and for the continuing presence of the Holy Spirit, he is asking for the renewal of fellowship (verse 11). He wants the chasm between God and himself to be bridged so there is once again oneness and unity. Perhaps David is remembering how the Spirit of God left King Saul (1 Samuel 16:14). David does not want the same thing to happen to him.

Refocus on the Future

Then David begins to focus on the future. In verse 12 he prays to be upheld by God's Spirit. Never again does he want to fail like

he failed with Bathsheba and Uriah. Never again does he want to fail himself in delaying the confession of his sin for so long. Perhaps you have experienced something similar to what David went through. Once you have confessed your sin and been restored to fellowship with God, you feel the need to make some new covenants with God, to drive a stake in the ground, and to purpose never to traverse the same territory again. You ask the Lord for new strength and power to resist temptation and sin. You ask for a fresh filling of His Spirit in order to be upheld in strength in the future. When we have been cleansed of sin and its guilt and shame, that is exactly what we should do.

David's experience at this time in the whole process of his restoration is best summarized in Psalm 32:1-2: "Blessed is he whose transgression is forgiven, whose sin is covered. Blessed is the man to whom the Lord does not impute iniquity, and in whose spirit there is no deceit." *Blessed* means "happy," or "contented." Happy, satisfied, and content is the man whose sin is forgiven by God and who is restored to fellowship with Him.

Studying about David's sin may have raised unpleasant memories in your own mind of past sins in your life. I hope you have been through the same process David went through. No matter what sin any Christian has committed, no matter what condemnation you may have felt, or what guilt and shame you may have experienced, blessed contentment can only come through confession, forgiveness, and restoration. Don't ever think you have sinned too greatly for God to forgive you. You see that He forgave the double sins of adultery and murder that David committed. And He will forgive your sins as well.

But you must come as David came: accepting responsibility, acknowledging the sinfulness of sin, and addressing your confession to God. If you do that, you will enjoy all that David did. Your sin will be removed, your joy restored, and your fellowship renewed. The giant of guilt will be defeated.

PERSONAL QUESTIONS

1. Turn to Psalms 32 and 51.

   a. What sins did David commit that led to his battle with guilt?

   b. When David left his sins unconfessed, what physical effect did it have on him? (Psalm 32:3)

   c. What state of emotion was he in? (Psalm 32:4)

   d. Whom could David talk to about his guilt, if anyone? Have you ever experienced this sort of secrecy with your own guilt?

   e. Whom, then, did God send to confront David? (See 2 Samuel 12:1-7.)

   f. What did David think of Nathan's story about the rich man and the poor man? (2 Samuel 12:5-6) What news did Nathan break to David? (2 Samuel 12:7)

g. Ultimately, what was David's response to his sin in Psalm 51? (See verse 4.) What pronouns does he use throughout the passage?

h. What does David acknowledge in Psalm 32:5?

i. How do you handle your sin? Do you live with the guilt or confess it to God?

j. After David admitted his sin, what did he ask of God in Psalm 51:2, 7, and 9?

k. As was with David, what is restored to us when we confess our sin? (Psalm 51:8, 11, 12)

2. Do you need to renew your fellowship with the Lord? What steps can you take today?

1. Review Psalms 32 and 51 and answer the following questions together.

   a. David was unable to talk to God about his sin. Discuss the effects this had on him. (See "The Agony of Guilt.")

   b. Why did God send Nathan to David? Discuss why God sometimes uses others to bring people to confession.

   c. In the story Nathan used to called David to account, whom did the poor man, rich man, and lamb each represent? (2 Samuel 12:1-7)

   d. In Psalm 32:5, what did David acknowledge? Why is it difficult to take responsibility for our sin?

e. Discuss how confession of past sins changed your life. If comfortable, share what was holding you back from confessing in the first place.

f. When we sin, whom are we ultimately sinning against? (Psalm 51:4)

g. Review the three steps to the complete removal of sin as mentioned in the section, "The Answer to Guilt."

h. After David confessed his sin and renewed his fellowship with God, what did he ask for? (Psalm 51:12)

2. Is there any sin too big that God cannot forgive? When we confess our sins, what are we, according to Psalm 32:1-2?

We are guilty and responsible for every sin we commit. But if we approach the Lord's Table in an unworthy manner, holding onto sin, we are then also found "guilty of the body and blood of the Lord" (1 Corinthians 11:27). This is a guilt that sinfully mocks the very One who died for your sins. So when you come to communion, be sure to examine yourself and make your confession before God, lest you dishonor Christ's sacrifice on your behalf.

SLAYING THE GIANT OF TEMPTATION

1 Corinthians 10:12-14

*In this lesson we discover how to recognize
and defeat a temptation to sin.*

OUTLINE

Some Christians feel they cannot resist temptation because they have
not learned God's secret for escaping the snares of sin: discovering
and taking the way of escape He provides.

I.   **The Common Experience of Temptation**

II. **The Controlled Environment of Temptation**

III. **The Certain Escape From Temptation**

IV. **Conclusion: How Do We Deal With Temptation?**
   A.   Recognize the Possibility of Temptation
   B.   Request Help in Advance of Temptation
   C.   Resist the Devil and He Will Flee From You
   D.   Retreat From Certain Kinds of Temptation
   E.   Remove Any Means of Sin Far From You
   F.   Replace Bad Influences With Good Ones
   G.   Resolve to Live on the High Road

Temptation is an ever-present factor in the life of every human being. From our forebears Adam and Eve down to the present day, the failure to resist temptation has been the source of countless tears of regret. The giant of temptation has captured the lives of many people. We must learn to defeat temptation if we are to walk victoriously in the spiritual life.

Thankfully, God has provided a way of escape from the giant of temptation. The apostle Paul wrote about that way in the passage of Scripture we will study in this lesson, 1 Corinthians 10:12-14. I don't know with certainty why Paul penned these specific words to the Christians living in Corinth, but it must have had something to do with the rampant wickedness in that city. Corinth was a seaport, a crossroads in the Mediterranean world and, as such, was home to every vice known to man. Paul may have written this particular part of his first letter to the church at Corinth to help them defeat the giant of temptation in their own lives.

That reasoning makes his words particularly applicable to us today. We live in a society not unlike Corinth. Every conceivable temptation flaunts itself daily in our culture, and far too many Christians have become statistics in the war against sin. We need Paul's words about escaping temptation as desperately as did the Corinthian believers.

Paul starts by helping us understand the commonality of temptation. No one is free from temptation, which means we must face it as a constant foe, no matter who we are.

THE COMMON EXPERIENCE OF TEMPTATION

Paul begins by saying that no Christian experiences a unique temptation; all temptation is common to man (verse 13). Somehow we get the idea that the temptations we face are unique, that no one else has ever faced the particular kind of pressure we feel. That is not true, Paul says. Temptation is the common enemy of every person on earth. There are no unique situations which would excuse us from the requirement to resist temptation and defeat it.

Scripture illustrates this truth from Genesis to Revelation. Abraham lied about his wife. Noah became intoxicated. David committed murder and adultery. Jonah rebelled against God. Peter denied the Lord Jesus. John Mark gave up on his missionary

commitment. Paul and Barnabas became cross with one another. And even the Lord Jesus Himself was tempted—just as we are. The important thing to remember from Jesus' temptation is that temptation is not sin. Though He was tempted, He was also without sin (Hebrews 4:15).

Temptation is exposure to the possibility of doing the wrong thing. Such exposure is not sin; it is not the same as doing the wrong thing, which is sin. The Bible offers no hope that temptation is going to go away, but it does offer hope for resisting temptation. In fact, the longer we walk with the Lord and grow in maturity, the more intense and subtle the temptations seem to become. Satan seems to work overtime in devising traps and devices by which we might fall. We will not kill the giant of temptation this side of heaven, but we can defeat him.

Kenneth Taylor, who wrote The Living Bible, paraphrased verse 13 like this: "Remember this—the wrong desires that come into your life aren't anything new and different. Many others have faced exactly the same problems before you." So remember that temptation is common to you, to me, and to every believer. It is to be expected, so let's prepare for it and plan for its defeat.

THE CONTROLLED ENVIRONMENT OF TEMPTATION

One of the greatest truths about temptation is found in the last part of verse 13. If every believer in Christ could internalize this truth, our battles with temptation would result in far more victories. Temptation occurs in an environment controlled by God; that is, the temptations God allows you to experience are not more than you can resist. You do not have to give in and sin.

God knows what our strength is, what our limitations are. Whenever I hear someone say, "It was more than I could handle," I know that is not true because the Word of God says all temptation is under God's control, and He does not give us more than we can resist with His help. A good example of this in Paul's life is the experience he described in 2 Corinthians 1:8-10. He described himself as being tested beyond his own strength, and yet not beyond God's ability to deliver him. That is the core truth of Scripture regarding temptation as stated in verse 13.

Most people would prefer that life be free of temptations. But here is what would happen if that were true: You would never be able to demonstrate your great love for the Lord Jesus Christ. You

would be kept from showing your loyalty to Almighty God and His holy principles as opposed to the things of the world. If we were simply automatons who were programmed to know God and to love God, God would receive no glory from our decisions to resist temptation and obey Him instead. When we resist temptation, God is glorified in our choices. Even though He gives us aid through the power of His Spirit, to resist or not is still our choice. And He is either glorified or not, depending on our choice.

THE CERTAIN ESCAPE FROM TEMPTATION

When we are tempted, God sees the end of the temptation (our escape) at the same time He sees the beginning of the temptation. When the test begins, God knows the way out (verse 13). He doesn't figure it out as we go along. Because Christ Himself was tempted, "He is able to aid those who are tempted" (Hebrews 2:18). He is able to come to our aid immediately when we are tempted because He has already "been there and done that." He knows the way of escape and has it ready for us.

One of the things I've learned over time is that temptation is not so much a matter of what we don't do as much as a matter of who we love. When we come to know the Lord Jesus, and we cultivate within our hearts a relationship of intimacy with Him, that in itself will keep us from many faults and many sins. His heroic image as the One who knew no sin becomes a powerful beacon for us. His ways of escape become ours through the indwelling of His Spirit. When we are living in fellowship with Him daily, it is hard to consider grieving Him, our Lord and best friend, by giving in to temptation. He becomes more than a preacher of do's and don'ts—He becomes the way of escape who is always with us.

One further admonition born of experience: With every temptation we ever face there is a point when we know the way of escape is before us. If we choose not to take it, it will not be there later. There is "a way" (singular) of escape. We must take it when God shows it to us. Not to take it is an indication that we didn't want to escape to begin with, which raises another level of concern about our desire to obey God in the first place.

The word "escape" which Paul uses was sometimes used in Greek to describe a very narrow passage through which one passed —like the steep walls of a canyon which defined a very narrow passage through a rugged bit of terrain. The way of escape is like

that. It is a single, narrow choice which must be made. There are no alternate ways out of that canyon of temptation. If we are going to get out, we have to take the one path that is provided. To turn and go a different way means being stuck in that place of temptation with no other escape.

Conclusion: How Do We Deal With Temptation?

Here are seven practical suggestions which I have found will help you choose the way of escape God provides and defeat the giant of temptation.

Recognize the Possibility of Temptation

The first indication that a person is setting himself up for a fall into sin is when he thinks he is beyond temptation. In verse 12, Paul states the case clearly: "Therefore let him who thinks he stands take heed lest he fall." The person who says, "That could never happen to me," is the most likely candidate to sin. "Pride goeth before destruction," says the King James Version (Proverbs 16:18).

A seminary professor who is a friend of mine kept track of ministers and students who failed in the ministry due to sexual temptation. When his list reached more than one hundred names, he suddenly realized the common element. In all but two cases, he said, those on the list had been characterized by pride. Woe to the person who pridefully believes he is immune from any temptation.

Request Help in Advance of Temptation

Twice our Lord taught His disciples about the power of prayer as a defense against temptation (Matthew 6:13; 26:41). Our daily prayer should be that God would protect us that day from the temptations which might enter our path. We should ask Him to make us sensitive, discerning, and aware of the very subtle traps the enemy might set. No soldier enters battle and then stops to sharpen his sword. Likewise, the best preparation for spiritual conflict is accomplished before the battle begins.

Resist the Devil and He Will Flee From You

James says that if we resist the devil, he will flee from us. But the prior condition for that resistance is our submission to God (James 4:7). A key factor in resisting the devil is to submit to the Word of God as Jesus did in resisting Satan's temptations in the wilderness (Matthew 4:1-11; Luke 4:1-14). At the end of that period,

when Jesus relied on verses from Deuteronomy to resist the devil's advances, the Bible says the devil "departed from Him." He will also depart from any believer who submits to the Word of God in resisting temptation.

Retreat From Certain Kinds of Temptation

Resisting temptation is always our responsibility, but how we do that can vary. One of the ways Scripture admonishes us to do that is to retreat—run from temptation. There are three kinds of temptation from which we should retreat quickly.

1. We Are to Retreat From Idolatry

   We are to flee from idolatry (1 Corinthians 10:14). An idol is anything that gets between you and God. While our idols may not be figurines sitting on a shelf in our home, there are certainly plenty of things which we are inclined to "worship" if given the opportunity. Flee from those things.

2. We Are to Retreat From Immorality

   Twice the New Testament commands us to flee from immorality (1 Corinthians 6:18; 2 Timothy 2:22). This is the most dangerous area of temptation because of the power of sexual attraction. It is a deception to think we can toy around with temptation in this area and come out unscathed. We are to imitate Joseph in the Old Testament who literally ran out of his master's house when he was being tempted by his master's wife—leaving his coat in her hands (Genesis 39)!

3. We Are to Retreat From Greed

   First Timothy 6:10-11 says we are to flee greed. The pursuit of material things, the never-ending temptation to seek more, more, more, is what Paul warns against in this passage. Material things can become idols which come between us and God. The lure for mammon is so strong that Paul says to flee from it.

Remove Any Means of Sin Far From You

We have a responsibility not to make ourselves available to temptation. One man who was trying to lose weight decided he would only stop at the bakery if God provided a parking place directly in front of the store. A space became available on his eighth trip around the block. That's not exactly demonstrating a high level of commitment to resisting temptation, is it? Yet how often do we find ourselves creating similar scenarios as we toy with temptation?

Romans 13:14 says to "make no provision for the flesh, to fulfill its lusts." Instead of setting ourselves up for failure, we should set ourselves up for victory. Don't put yourself in a position where it's impossible not to sin. Put yourself in a place where it's not possible to sin by removing the means of sin far from you.

Replace Bad Influences With Good Ones

Proverbs 13:20 says, "He who walks with wise men will be wise, but the companion of fools will be destroyed." There is a definite tension involved in our lives as believers. On one hand we want to spend our time around godly people who will influence us and move us in the direction of maturity in Christ. On the other hand, if Christians are the only people we spend time with, how will non-Christians be won to Christ? The records of history are replete with multitudes of cases of well-meaning Christians being diverted from their standards of holiness in Christ by temptations encountered in their relationships with non-Christians. We must maintain accountability with other believers who can help us monitor our relationships. Who is having the most influence? Am I influencing this person for Christ, or is this person influencing me toward the world and sin?

It is obviously the right thing to do to reach out to those who don't know Christ, or even Christians who are less mature and still struggling to overcome the world. But if you become trapped in a web of deceit and sin because of your involvement, it needs to stop until you can regain perspective and maintain accountability for your own life and standards in Christ. You need to replace bad influences with good ones.

Resolve to Live on the High Road

If you are a Christian, you need to resolve to get off the low road of non-commitment and live permanently on the high road. The high road is not free of temptation or spiritual pitfalls, but it is the road by which you are committed to taking the way of escape God provides in times of testing. You will be tested, and there will be a way of escape provided. But only those on the high road will see it and take it.

Why not decide today to be a Christian committed to defeating the giant of temptation? God has promised a way out of every test, but it still requires a choice from you in every instance. Choose the way God provides, and the giant of temptation will flee. That's a promise from God Himself.

PERSONAL QUESTIONS

1. Turn to 1 Corinthians 10:12-14.

   a. What do we learn about temptation in verse 13?

   b. Is temptation a sin? Though Christ was tempted, what did He not do? (See Hebrews 4:15.)

   c. What does God not allow when it comes to temptation? (verse 13)

   d. According to Hebrews 2:18, why is Jesus able to aid the tempted?

   e. What does the knowledge that Christ came to endure all things and provide a way of escape in temptation make you want to do?

   f. What are we to recognize about temptation? What attitude should we take up to avoid falling? (verse 12)

2. Read Matthew 26:41.

   a. What two things does Jesus tell us to do? Why?

   b. The spirit is _____, but the flesh is _____.

   c. Why do you think the flesh wins out over the spirit so often? How can prayer combat this tendency and give the spirit the victory?

3. Read James 4:7.

   a. What are we to do toward God?

   b. What are we to do toward the devil? What will he do in turn?

   c. The next time you are tempted, what will you do? To whom will you turn?

GROUP QUESTIONS

1. As a group, read 1 Corinthians 10:12-14.

   a. What is common among all men? (verse 13)

   b. Even who was tempted? But what did He not do? (Hebrews 4:15)

   c. Though we are exposed to temptation, what does God provide for each of us? (verse 13)

   d. What does Paul say about being tested in 2 Corinthians 1:8-10?

   e. How should our relationship with Christ look if we want to avoid giving in to sin?

   f. Has there ever been a moment in your life when you could see God's way of escape before you? If comfortable, share with the group.

2. What do Matthew 6:13 and 26:41 tell us to do when temptation presents itself to us?

3. What kinds of temptation are we to avoid according to the following verses?

    a. 1 Corinthians 10:14

    b. 1 Corinthians 6:18; 2 Timothy 2:22

    c. 1 Timothy 6:10-11

4. What types of relationships are we called to have in Proverbs 13:20?

    a. Is it wrong to have friendships with non-Christians? Why or why not? When should we avoid spending time with those who don't know Christ?

    b. Is there someone in your life who does not know Christ? Discuss how you can best influence them, rather than them influencing you.

DID YOU KNOW?

J esus gave the ultimate example in combating temptation during His forty days in the wilderness (Luke 4:1-14). Satan pounced on Him with clever arguments, but Jesus annihilated every temptation with the Word of God. It is interesting to note that every verse Jesus quoted came from Deuteronomy, a book we often have trouble plodding through. But if our Lord and Savior was able to use that obscure book to combat the devil himself, we should be even more vigilant about inscribing the entirety of the Word of God in our hearts (2 Timothy 3:16-17).

SLAYING THE GIANT OF ANGER

Ephesians 4:25-32

*In this lesson we learn how to keep the emotion
of anger from becoming sinful.*

OUTLINE

The Christian community has heard so much about the destructive
effects of anger that the non-sinful expression of this emotion has
been overlooked. The Bible doesn't say, "Don't be angry." Rather, it
says, "Don't let your anger become sinful and hurtful."

I. **Recognizing Sinless Anger**

II. **Renouncing Sinful Anger**
   A. Don't Nurse Your Anger
   B. Don't Rehearse Your Anger
   C. Don't Converse About Your Anger
   D. Don't Disperse Your Anger
   E. Do Reverse Your Anger

Early in the 1970s a promising young American pianist gave a concert in the chamber music room of the Erewan Hotel in Bangkok. A few moments into his opening piece, he discovered that a certain key on the piano—one critical to the piece he was playing—was sticking. In addition, the piano stool had been oiled so excessively that he was constantly spinning around and facing the audience. Without stopping his first piece, he transitioned to his next number only to discover that another key began to stick. To try to loosen the keys he began kicking on the bottom side of the piano, which caused one of the legs to give way, slanting the piano toward the floor. Too frustrated to continue playing, he marched off stage and reappeared with an ax with which he began to chop the piano to pieces. He stopped only when restrained by police.

It is safe to say that what the audience witnessed that night was a full-blown temper tantrum—anger in full bloom. Anger is among the most frequently cited spiritual giants we see stalking about in modern culture. And it seems its expression is on the rise. Today we have people shooting each other on the freeway in America over incidents that ten years ago would have just produced an expletive or two. People feel no hesitancy today in taking out their rage against another person in ways that end up sending them to jail or prison. Anger for many people is an uncontrollable emotion.

Ironically, anger can often do more harm to the person who expresses it than to the person who is on the receiving end of it. Someone has said, "Anger is an acid that can do more harm to the vessel in which it is stored than to the person on whom it is poured." Therefore, there are two reasons to learn how to defeat the giant of anger: to protect both the person who is angry as well as the person toward whom anger is directed.

Ephesians 4:25-32 is a key passage in Paul's epistles that will help us identify, and defeat, the giant of anger.

RECOGNIZING SINLESS ANGER

Paul says something in verse 26 which will surprise many Christians: "Be angry, and do not sin." The implication is, of course, that there is an anger which is not sin. It is possible to be angry without sinning. Anger has such a negative connotation that many people assume it is always sinful to be angry.

Before we clarify what Paul is saying, let's make sure we understand this: Paul is not giving permission here for the venting of frustration and rage. That is not the permissible anger he is talking about. Getting one's anger out is a popular theme in pop psychology today, but it has no biblical basis. For instance, in the New Living Translation, Jesus' words in Matthew 5:22 are rendered this way: "But I say, if you are even angry with someone, you are subject to judgment!" Paul says anger is a work of the flesh (Galatians 5:19-21), and Proverbs says it is a fool who vents all his feelings (Proverbs 29:11). I have even read that secular thinkers are reconsidering the idea that venting anger is helpful. Studies indicate that venting one's rage only makes one angrier and solidifies those negative emotions.

So what is Paul referring to when he says to be angry, but do not sin? The answer is found in the life of the Lord Jesus Christ. There was more than one occasion on which He expressed anger, yet we know that He lived without sin. Therefore He wasn't manifesting self-centered rage or hostile venom toward others. Whatever He was doing, He was being angry without sinning.

The clearest expression of Jesus' anger is recorded in John 2:14-15 when He drove the merchants and money changers out of the temple in Jerusalem. To understand why Jesus did what He did, we have to understand what was happening in the temple. The money changers and merchants were extortionists, cheating poor pilgrims out of their money. When Israelites came to the temple to offer a sacrifice, the animals they brought would be disapproved by the temple officials. They would be forced to purchase "approved" animals at an inflated price from the corrupt merchants and money changers. Jesus' anger was first directed at the injustice toward temple worshipers.

Secondly, Jesus was so angry because worship of God was being obstructed by the booths and tables set up in the Court of the Gentiles. This area of the temple was for Gentiles who wanted to worship the true God. They couldn't get near because the Court of the Gentiles had been turned into a mall of animal sellers and money changers.

How was Jesus' anger different from ours? His anger was never about His own "stuff"—His own agenda, His own schedule, His own rights, His own preferences, His own desires. That's what our anger is almost always about. His anger was over injustice and unrighteousness as manifested in the temple of Israel. That is the sort of righteous anger acceptable to God, and it is not sinful. It would not hurt for Christians to express more of a similar kind of righteous anger toward the injustices in our world today.

On another occasion Jesus became angry at the Pharisees in a synagogue because they accused Him of healing someone on the Sabbath (Mark 3:5). They were more concerned about the letter of the Law than they were about the spirit of the Law. They were more concerned with tradition than they were with compassion.

There is an anger that is righteous and not sinful. But it is always directed at the abuse of righteousness and justice and love and compassion. It is not used as a tool of retribution when we don't get our own way.

RENOUNCING SINFUL ANGER

In the same text (verse 26), there is also a kind of anger that is sinful—an anger which is not to be nurtured or condoned lest the devil see an opportunity to arouse bitterness and resentment in our lives. That kind of anger, Paul says later in verse 31, is to be put away from the believer's life. Sinful anger is by far the kind of anger that we are tempted to express most often. Here are some ways to avoid being defeated by the giant of sinful anger.

Don't Nurse Your Anger

When Paul says not to let the sun go down on our anger, he is saying, "Don't nurse your anger." Don't protect it and coddle it, giving it an ongoing place to live in your life. Be done with it in short order. While sundown is used here as a figure of speech, it is an excellent way to assess the state of your anger. If there is something you've been angry about during the day, make sure you put an end to it by the end of the day. Don't sleep on your anger—especially if your anger has been directed toward your spouse.

When we choose not to get rid of our anger, the danger is that it will become something worse than anger. Anger turns into resentment, and resentment turns into bitterness, and bitterness turns into unforgiveness, and unforgiveness turns into a defiled conscience. Pretty soon, we have become captives of our own anger. We can't think about anything except the person or issue which is the target of our anger. But if we release our anger by confessing it to the Lord and settling accounts if necessary with another person, we avoid the prison we were on the verge of creating for ourselves.

Let bedtime be a reminder: Am I nursing sinful anger toward anyone or anything?

Don't Rehearse Your Anger

Secondly, don't rehearse your anger. Some people love to tell others how angry they are. Henry Brandt used to say that when a person says to someone, "You make me so angry," they are saying something that isn't true. No one can make you angry. If you express sinful anger, it is only because there is anger in you already. If another person does something that draws that anger out of you, the anger is not their fault—it's yours. If there was no anger in you to begin with, they could do the same thing and it would produce no sinful response in you at all. No one can cause us to become something which we are not.

When we verbalize our anger to another person, all we are doing is confirming it, making our convictions deeper: "Yes, I am angry. That person has hurt me. The more I say it, the more I know I'm right." Verbalizing our anger just makes the roots of that anger go deeper and deeper into our heart. And the deeper the roots go, the harder it is to dig that anger out when you finally do realize you need to stop it. Don't make anger a part of your conversation. Like an actor, the more you rehearse the part, the more natural it becomes for you to play it.

Don't Converse About Your Anger

This is almost the same as not rehearsing your anger. While rehearsing your anger is done for the purpose of convincing and justifying yourself, conversing about your anger to others takes the form of corrupt communication coming out of your mouth (verse 29).

In the New Testament, the word *corrupt* was the word for "cutting." Paul is saying don't let words which have a cutting effect come out of your mouth. Americans have almost made a sport out of sarcastic, cynical, cutting forms of speech. Because it is so prevalent in our culture, it is easy to pick it up without even realizing it. That is not to blame the culture. We Christians are to blame for not practicing and obeying the Word of God. I believe Christians should purpose to remove sarcasm altogether from their vocabulary because of the danger of setting off a cycle of that kind of speech between two people once it is begun.

I recall learning a lesson about this kind of speech with a friend of mine. We would get together often for lunch, and good-naturedly rib each other, cut one another down, the way friends will often do. But suddenly my friend stopped being available for lunch; he would

hardly acknowledge me when we were around one another. And so I went to him to find out what was wrong. It turns out something I had said in one of our sarcasm sessions had lodged in his heart and hurt him deeply. After we reconciled our relationship, I purposed that I would never run the risk of damaging another person with "corrupt" cutting speech again.

Anger can fuel cutting communication. You can find yourself saying corrupt things about or to another person if you are harboring anger in your heart. Don't allow anger to fuel cutting conversation. The kind of speech we are to be characterized by is edifying speech, words that impart grace to the hearers (verse 29). Words that build up another person cannot be fueled by anger. Therefore we are to put anger aside.

Here's one final point about conversation fueled or characterized by anger. If you associate with people who speak this way, you run the risk of speaking that way yourself (Proverbs 22:24-25). I don't like to be around angry people, and I hope you don't either on an ongoing basis. It's very difficult to be around that kind of person without becoming that kind of person yourself.

Don't Disperse Your Anger

Fourth, don't disperse your anger—nor your bitterness, wrath, clamor, evil speaking, or malice (verse 31). Sinful anger is just one of a number of sinful responses and behaviors that is not to proceed from the life of a Christian, a person controlled by the Holy Spirit.

To use modern language, I think Paul is talking here about a person who throws a temper tantrum when he can't get what he wants. Since my children are all grown, it's been many, many years since I've seen anything close to a temper tantrum. But more recently I've seen my grandchildren have a fit just because they can't get what they want, how they want it, and when they want it. Even if they were old enough to talk clearly, they couldn't explain why they were so angry. They were just mad! And they were dispersing that anger onto everyone who happened to be around.

Anger is nothing more than a sophisticated version of a temper tantrum. Just because we can define it with eloquent speech doesn't mean it is any more justified. We are still mad that we can't get what we want. And our anger overflows out of us and defiles everyone around us.

Instead of nursing, rehearsing, conversing about, and dispersing our anger, we need to reverse our anger before it hurts us and others.

Do Reverse Your Anger

How do you reverse anger? Paul says you do it with forgiveness and lovingkindness and tenderness (verse 32). You go to the person toward whom you have directed your anger and you minister to that person.

Paul says in Romans 12:20, "If your enemy is hungry, feed him; if he is thirsty, give him a drink; for in so doing you will heap coals of fire on his head." What does it mean to heap coals of fire upon someone's head? This expression grew out of an Egyptian custom. When a person had done something wrong, in order for him to express his contrition and shame for what he had done, he would place a pan of hot coals on his head to express the burning shame within his heart. So Paul says when we do good to those who have done us evil, when we go to that person and we show them love and tenderness, we put coals of fire upon their heads. We in essence shame them because of what they have done to us. We reverse what they have done to us by doing good to them.

So how do you reverse your anger? How do you heap burning coals upon the head of a person toward whom you have been angry and who may have in fact done something to hurt you? See if you can figure out some way to demonstrate love toward him. But note: The point is not to shame the person. That still has an element of self in it. The point is simply to love him. If shame arises, it will do so on its own when sin comes face-to-face with pure love. We are to love others in the way that God in Christ has loved us.

Is there someone today at whom you are angry? Slay the giant. A tender action of forgiving love is a weapon the giant of anger cannot withstand.

1. Read Ephesians 4:25-32.

   a. What is Paul implying in verse 26 when he says, "Be angry, and do not sin"?

   b. What example do we have of sinless anger in John 2:14-15?

   c. Why was Jesus' anger sinless? Whom or what was His anger directed toward?

   d. In verses 26-27, what are we not to do with our anger?

   e. Are you nursing any anger currently? What is the danger in holding on to our anger?

   f. What does Paul say about corrupt, cutting words in verse 29? What kind of speech should we have instead?

   g. Do you tend to speak with sarcasm? If so, why do you speak that way? Have your words ever cut someone down?

   h. By whom are we sealed? (verse 30) How can this help us when we feel anger building inside us?

   i. Have you ever caught yourself throwing a temper tantrum of sorts? As Christians, what are we to put away? (verse 31) Is this a difficult task for you? Why or why not?

   j. If someone hurts us, what does Paul recommend we do in turn? Who forgave us for our wrongdoings? (verse 32)

2. How can you determine this week to move on from any anger you may feel?

1. Review Ephesians 4:25-32 as a group.

   a. What kind of anger is not sinful? Discuss Jesus' anger in John 2:14-15. Why was His anger justified?

   b. What does Paul mean when he says, "Do not let the sun go down on your wrath"?

   c. What does anger often turn into when we nurse it? Share about a time when your anger turned into something more. What should you have done with that anger instead?

   d. What does verbalizing our anger do to our hearts?

   e. Is our culture to blame for the anger we feel? Instead of blaming our environment, what can we do instead? (verses 29, 31-32)

2. Read Proverbs 22:24-25.

   a. We are admonished not to be friends with whom? (verse 24)

   b. Why would spending time with such people be a bad idea? (verse 25)

   c. What would it do for our soul? Interpret verse 25 together.

3. Turn to Proverbs 29:11.

    a. What does a fool do? What does a wise man do?

    b. Think of a time when you wish you were silent but were not. Now think of a time when you held your tongue. Share how the adage of the fool and wise man fits your personal experiences.

DID YOU KNOW?

Anger is found in the stories and lives of many of the Bible's most prominent characters. Cain became extremely angry with his brother Abel (Genesis 4:5) and eventually committed the world's first murder. Moses had an anger problem as well, and he too killed a man because of it (Exodus 2:12). Jonah became angry with God after the people of Nineveh turned from their wicked ways and repented of their sins (Jonah 4:1). In fact, he told God in Jonah 4:9 that he was "angry, even to death!"

SLAYING THE GIANT OF RESENTMENT

Selected Scriptures

*In this lesson we learn practical strategies
for remaining free of resentment.*

OUTLINE

When people find themselves in a full-blown state of bitterness or
rebellion, they are bearing the fruit of a tiny seed called resentment.
Not to uproot resentment when it first appears is to make probable
a more serious bout with bitterness down the road.

   I.   **The Examination of Resentment**

  II.   **The Example of Resentment**

 III.   **The Expense of Resentment**

  IV.   **Five Steps to Winning Against the Giant of Resentment**
        A. Think It Through
        B. Write It Down
        C. Work It Out
        D. Talk It Over
        E. Give It Up

Americans have often been shocked by incidents of random shooting in which innocent people have been killed or wounded. People are sometimes afraid to turn on the television or radio for fear of encountering another news story of this kind. In almost all of these cases, those who knew the perpetrator were in complete shock that the person would commit such a horrible act of violence. Often the person had no former criminal record, had raised no one's suspicions as far as being "on the edge" of violence, and appeared to be a responsible citizen.

However, once an investigation begins into the background of a person who commits explosive acts of violence against others, it is not unusual for a pattern of seething resentments to emerge. Resentment bubbles and boils beneath the surface of a calm demeanor, ticking like a time bomb. The trouble is that no one, often not even the person himself, knows when the bomb will go off. Like the straw that breaks the camel's back, one final act which brings forth yet more resentment can set off violent acts.

Resentment may be among the most deceptive of the giants hiding in the forest of our lives. Unlike anger, which is more impulsive and sudden, resentment builds slowly and gradually over time. No one feeling of resentment is enough to trigger dangerous behavior; but add up feelings of resentment over time, and you have a volatile situation. And because resentment can be masked by an outwardly calm exterior, often it goes undetected by others. Accumulated resentment can lead in time to anger and bitterness—and yes, even to violence.

The giant of resentment needs to be banished immediately from our lives when it is first detected. Step one is to make sure we know what resentment is and how to detect its presence.

THE EXAMINATION OF RESENTMENT

We have to discover the meaning of resentment through the back door of the Greek language. The English word is not actually used in the New Testament, but the Greek word *logizomai* underlies what we refer to as resentment. An example of this is found in a negative context in the great love chapter of the Bible, 1 Corinthians 13. There Paul says that love "thinks no evil" (verse 5).

Logizomai has its roots in the concept of bookkeeping. It means "to calculate" or "to reckon." Entering a number into a ledger for

the purpose of keeping track of it is what is meant by *logizomai*. The word is used to our benefit when it describes how God does not enter into His ledger a record of the sin of the person who is in Christ (Romans 4:8; 2 Corinthians 5:19). Paul also expressed hope that the failures of some in their actions toward him would not be recorded against them (2 Timothy 4:16).

While there are many situations in which record keeping is essential, in personal relationships it is not only unnecessary but harmful. Love, Paul says, does not take into account wrongs that are suffered. Love doesn't write down and keep records of wrongs that are done. Love looks for a chance to erase the record of wrongs at every opportunity, to forgive and keep a clean slate.

THE EXAMPLE OF RESENTMENT

We find a sad example of resentment in the Old Testament Scriptures. When King David was dying, he brought Solomon, his son, before him and gave him some instructions. David still bore in his memory resentment over the actions of Joab, one of his military commanders. Joab had unlawfully killed two commanders in the army on the basis of his own resentments, and David had not forgotten it. David had remembered Joab's actions for years but had never avenged the deaths of his two commanders by killing Joab. So David called Solomon in and corrupted his mind by commanding that Joab not be allowed to die a natural death. In other words, David wanted Solomon to kill Joab (1 Kings 2:5-6). David had nurtured his resentment for years and finally decided to act on it.

The trouble with resentment is that it is not static—it does not remain the same. Resentment is like a cancer that grows ever so slowly, eating away at the insides of the person who nurtures it. And, like cancer, ultimately other people become involved. Some people say, "If I want to be bitter and resentful, that's my business." But, as Hebrews 12:15 points out, bitterness is a root that springs up and defiles many people in the process. Regardless of how benign you think your resentment is, it is not. Resentment is an evil root that is growing daily, waiting only for the opportunity to bring forth its fruit.

THE EXPENSE OF RESENTMENT

Experts agree that the one who nurtures resentment pays a high price to do so, both psychologically and physically. As I have mentioned earlier in these studies, doctors are documenting more

and more instances in which anger, bitterness, and unforgiveness are the causative factors in physical diseases. S. I. McMillan, in his 1963 book *None of These Diseases*, says the estimates vary from sixty to one hundred percent. Hypertension and heart disease are major illnesses influenced by the stress brought about by unforgiveness.

Psychologically we are imprisoned by our past. We think we have put another person under our control by our unwillingness to forgive, but it is really we who become the slaves of resentment. We become the embodiment of our resentment. Our life revolves around that which we refuse to let go of. Lewis Smedes, in his 1984 book *Forgive and Forget*, tells a story which illustrates how a person's whole life can be bound up in his resentment. It is a story from a play based on World War II war crimes. A German officer was sentenced to prison for his part in wartime atrocities. Upon his release, he and his wife planned to live out their lives quietly in a cabin in the countryside.

A French journalist whose entire family had been killed under orders of the German officer, had waited all the years the officer was in prison to extract vengeance. The court had not sentenced the officer to death, but the journalist had in his own heart. He stirred up resentment and hatred in a group of people who agreed to join him in putting the officer and his wife to death. On the afternoon of the planned killing, the journalist went to interview the officer and ended up revealing who he was, telling the German the story of his family. The journalist, upon meeting the aged officer, was suddenly softened by the man's difficult station in life and warned him that a mob was coming that night to kill him. He offered to lead the officer through the woods to safety.

The officer agreed to go on one condition: that the journalist forgive him—which he could not do. The journalist left and returned that night with the mob and killed the officer and his wife. He was willing to lead a person to safety whom he was not able to forgive. To forgive the officer would have meant giving up his whole reason for living. He had spent so many years focused on what the German officer had done to his family that to give that up would have meant giving up the purpose of his life.

Resentment exacts a high price from any who would choose to possess it. For those who want to live free from resentment, five steps are critical.

Five Steps to Winning Against the Giant of Resentment

Think It Through

First, it is important to step back from the trees and try to get a picture of the whole forest. Just as we get so absorbed in reading a book or watching a movie or working on a hobby that we lose track of time, so we can lose track of the destructive nature of resentment. Do we really want to stay committed to something as destructive and harmful as resentment?

In all the research I have done on resentment, there seems to be one dominating reason why people engage in it: Resentment gives people a feeling of superiority over the person toward whom their hate is directed. It makes them feel as if they are the righteous person who has been ill-treated by a lesser person. They enjoy fantasizing their plots of revenge. They mentally rehearse the story to themselves over and over, etching the details further into their memory with each retelling. Someone has said that resentment gives us two things: neurotic pleasure and religious pride.

Think it through! Is this what you are doing? Is it worth it to enjoy this sordid pleasure and risk your own health?

Write It Down

Write down why you are filled with resentment. I have discovered through counseling that often, when you ask a person consumed with resentment and unforgiveness to tell you why he is, he can't give a clear reason. Over time, the resentment has taken on a life of its own independent of what initially caused it.

If you will write down on a piece of paper in simple terms why you are resentful and read it out loud to yourself, it will sound totally different to you than it does when you rehearse it in your mind. Not only will it sound different, it won't have the emotion attached to it that you feel when you think about it. If you are honest, it will sound far less justifiable; that is, there is something that happens to facts after being swirled around in the poison of resentment over time. They grow in size and seriousness. They get blown out of proportion. Reducing those facts back to their original size and shape by putting them on a plain piece of paper will help you regain perspective.

When you complete the following single sentence, "I am filled with resentment because . . . ," do it when you're alone. Why? I predict

that you will be a bit embarrassed when you discover that what is written on the paper is what you are so upset about.

Work It Out

A man who had been married for fifty years to the same woman was asked the secret of their marital bliss. "Well," he said, "it's kind of like this. When my wife and I got married, we made an agreement that whenever she was bothered about something, she would just tell me off and get it out of her system. And if I ever got mad at her about something, I would take a walk. I guess you can attribute our marital success to the fact that I have largely led an outdoor life."

I'm not suggesting you can overpower anger with exercise. But there is a significant amount of research that suggests people who get regular physical exercise handle conflicts better than those who don't. Because most of us don't have jobs that are physically demanding, we have to create that situation artificially through exercise. Exhausting oneself with work or exercise seems to take an edge off of our emotions and helps to keep us "drained" of pent up feelings. It's not a cure-all (nor should it be interpreted as a recommendation to vent your rage on a punching bag), but exercise is as good for your soul as it is for your body.

Talk It Over

If you are a Christian, I know one of your friends—the Lord Jesus Christ. So I want to suggest to you that you talk over your resentments with Him in prayer. Perhaps you should read to Him what you wrote down on the piece of paper. Just tell Him, "Lord, here is why I feel resentful toward so-and-so." Then tell Him. You're not going to shock Him—He knows how you feel already. And it will begin a conversation that will hopefully lead you in resolving your resentment before it goes further and deeper.

I have read how missionaries learn to get leeches off their skin— by soaking in a warm bath of balsam. If they try to simply pull the leeches off, part of the leech will remain hooked in the skin and cause an infection. But in the warm bath, they unhook themselves and can be pulled off cleanly. Bathing in the grace of God in the presence of Jesus has the same effect on resentment. It is hard to remain bitter and resentful while sitting in the presence of the Lord in prayer. Resentment will unhook itself from your heart, and you'll find yourself able to lay it down. When you begin to ponder what the Lord has done for you, how He has forgiven your every sin and holds no resentments toward you when you sin against

Him, you will begin to see the hypocrisy of holding resentments against others.

If you haven't accepted the forgiveness God offers for your own sins, it's much easier to hold on to your resentments toward others. But if you are a child of God who has been cleansed of sin against whom God holds no grudges, you should find yourself unable to maintain your resentment and unforgiveness toward others. We are to forgive others as God in Christ has forgiven us (Ephesians 4:32). And there is no better time to be reminded of that fact than when you are talking over your resentments with Him.

Give It Up

Clara Barton, founder of the American Red Cross, was once reminded of an especially cruel thing that someone had done to her years before—but she didn't seem to recall it. And her friend said, "Don't you remember?" Clara Barton said, "No, I distinctly remember forgetting it."

Did you know the only part of the Lord's Prayer that is repeated is the part about forgiveness? "Forgive us our debts, as we forgive our debtors," and clear at the end as an addendum to the prayer is this statement from Matthew that says, "For if you forgive men their trespasses, your heavenly Father will also forgive you. But if you do not forgive men their trespasses, neither will your Father forgive your trespasses" (Matthew 6:12, 14-15).

God's method for getting rid of resentments is through forgiveness. The Bible tells us that we are to love our enemies, bless those who curse us, do good to those who hate us, and pray for those who spitefully use us and persecute us. If we do this, it says, we will demonstrate that we are truly children of God. We are to act like our Heavenly Father. That's the only way I can explain some of the forgiveness I have heard about.

If you are nurturing some level of resentment toward a person or situation in your life, I urge you to work through the five steps above—and give it up. Your life free from the giant of resentment will be far sweeter and healthier in every respect.

1. Read 1 Corinthians 13:5. At the end of this verse, what does Paul say about love?

2. According to 2 Corinthians 5:19, what did God in Christ do for us? What did He not do?

    a. What did He commit to us? What do you think that means?

    b. How can you apply this verse to your own life? Is there any resentment building in you that you need to let go of?

3. Read Hebrews 12:15. What should we be careful of in our relationships with others?

    a. How can this behavior affect other people's spiritual lives?

    b. How can bitterness and resentment affect the one who nurtures them? Has bitterness ever had a negative effect on you? In what way?

4. Why do you think people allow resentment into their hearts? What is the underlying cause?

    a. Have you ever written down your resentments? Why do you think it is helpful to do so?

    b. Is there a special exercise routine you have to help with your anger? Have you noticed any positive results from that exercise?

    c. Who is the most important Friend we can turn to when we start to feel resentful? What is so important to remember about God and His grace?

1. Review what Paul says about love in 1 Corinthians 13:5.

   a. Discuss what the word *logizomai* means.

   b. What does God not do according to Romans 4:8 and 2
      Corinthians 5:19? Is there anyone you're keeping a record of
      wrongs against? Share if comfortable.

2. In 1 Kings 2:5-6, who wronged David?

   a. What did David ask of his son Solomon?

   b. What happens over time to the resentment that sits in us?

3. Discuss the story Lewis Smedes told in his book *Forgive and Forget*
   and the effects resentment had on the French journalist's life.

4. What are the five steps to winning against the giant of
   resentment?

   a. Why is it necessary to think through our resentment? What
      negative effects can resentment have in our own lives?

b. Discuss why we might harbor resentment against someone in the first place.

c. Has anyone in the group written down their feelings of resentment in the past? How did it help in the process of defeating this giant?

d. What positive effects does sitting in the presence of Jesus have on resentment?

5. According to Matthew 6:12, 14-15, what is God's method of getting rid of resentment? How can each of you apply this to your own life?

DID YOU KNOW?

One of the Bible's greatest stories of reconciliation was born out of a great sense of resentment. Do you remember how Jacob literally stole the birthright blessing of his older brother Esau (Genesis 27:35)? Esau became so angry that he plotted to kill his own brother (Genesis 27:41). So Jacob fled for his life and did not see Esau for many years. When they finally met again, Jacob was terrified and bowed down to him. But in a moving scene of compassion, Esau ran to see his estranged brother, and they embraced one another and wept (Genesis 33:4).

SLAYING THE GIANT OF DOUBT

John 20:24-29

In this lesson we learn strategies for overcoming doubt.

OUTLINE

Doubt can work for us or work against us. Negatively speaking, doubt can make us cynical and keep us from discovering truth. On the positive side, doubt can motivate us to dig deep and uncover that which will confirm truths long believed but lately questioned.

I. Facing the Giant of Doubt
   A. Doubt Develops in Isolation
   B. Doubt Demands Evidence
   C. Doubt Draws Us Back to Christ
   D. Doubt Deepens Our Faith
   E. Doubt Defines Our Faith

II. Fighting the Giant of Doubt
   A. Admit Your Doubts Personally
   B. Articulate Your Doubts Clearly
   C. Acknowledge Your Doubts Prayerfully
   D. Analyze the Evidence Diligently
   E. Accept the Limitations Humbly
   F. Adjust to the Universe's Complexity

On February 15, 1947, an Avianca Airline flight bound for Quito, Ecuador, slammed into the side of 14,000-foot El Tablazo, a mountain peak not far from Bogotá, Colombia. On that flight (there were no survivors) was a young New Yorker named Glenn Chambers. He was flying to Quito, Ecuador, to fulfill a life-long dream of becoming a missionary.

Before leaving the Miami airport earlier that day, Glenn had written a last note to mail to his mother. He had grabbed the only piece of paper he could find nearby, part of an advertisement that had the searching word WHY printed across the top. By the time his mother received that note in the mail, Glenn Chambers was dead. His mother asked "WHY?" concerning her son's death, as have countless others throughout history. Reconciling the "badness" of life with the goodness of God is only one of many reasons people sometimes have doubts.

The giant of doubt loves nothing better than a complex situation, such as the death of a family member, to step in and tempt us to wonder if we're right about God after all. Doubts are not sin. But if doubts are not managed and handled appropriately, they can lead to despair —or worse. In this lesson, we study a situation in which a man named Thomas came face-to-face with the object of his own doubts. From his experience, we can derive principles which will help us manage our own doubts and do so in a way that will strengthen, not weaken, our faith.

Doubt is not new in the spiritual experience of people who know and trust God. David and the other psalmists regularly cried out with uncertainty to God. Solomon wrote a whole book, Ecclesiastes, on what he considered the uncertainty of the reality we live in and around each day. And in the New Testament, John the Baptist was up front with his doubts, asking Jesus plainly, "Are You the Coming One, or do we look for another?" (Matthew 11:3) And this after he had baptized Jesus Himself in the Jordan River, seeing the dove descend from heaven upon Him, and hearing the Father proclaim that Jesus was His beloved Son (Matthew 3:16-17)!

The giant of doubt would love to move you from doubt to unbelief. But by applying the principles of this lesson, you will learn to ask and get answers for those issues of faith which arise in every Christian's walk from time to time.

Facing the Giant of Doubt

John 20 records the story of the greatest doubter in the Bible, Thomas—a disciple of Jesus. From what I can gather about Thomas in Scripture, he appears to have been a melancholy sort—what we might call a pessimist today (John 11:16; 14:5). That's not altogether a bad trait. Melancholy people sometimes make good quality control experts because they're the first to spot the flaws or mistakes. They're always looking for proof. And being a doubter doesn't mean Thomas was an unbeliever. He apparently had been a faithful member of Jesus' band of twelve disciples. In fact, tradition suggests that it was Thomas who carried the Christian faith to India after the resurrection of Christ.

But it was the Resurrection that caused him to stumble. He had a hard time believing that Jesus was raised from the dead. Let's track Thomas' experience and see how his doubts were ultimately answered.

Doubt Develops in Isolation

After the Resurrection, Jesus appeared to the disciples in a room where they had gathered. Apparently everyone was there except Thomas. We don't know why he was absent, but he was (verse 24). Without speculating about what we don't know, let me set forth a principle that is true regardless of whether it was true of Thomas: Doubt flourishes in isolation. When you are separated from others who have strong faith, your faith can grow weaker. John the Baptist began to have his doubts about Jesus when he was isolated and alone in jail.

We can be isolated in more than a physical sense; we can also find ourselves isolated emotionally. I have found it to be profitable to take my emotional temperature whenever I find doubts coming into my mind. Sometimes if we are ill, or feeling discouraged, or we're separated from family and friends, doubts can find their way into our thinking much more easily. One of my favorite sayings is that "our souls and our bodies live so close together, they catch each other's diseases." And C. S. Lewis, the brilliant British apologist, said he struggled seriously with doubts when he was on a trip and found himself alone in a hotel room, separated from family and friends.

So be forewarned—isolation is a breeding ground for doubts.

Doubt Demands Evidence

In verse 25, Thomas won't take the word of the other disciples concerning Jesus' resurrection. He demands proof. He wants to see the nailprints in His hands and the spear wound in His side. It was

Thomas who had warned the disciples about going to Jerusalem, fearing they would all be killed. And now that his fear has been realized, he finds it hard to believe that Jesus' death has been reversed —that He is alive.

The Church has been hard on Thomas throughout history for his doubts. But I wonder if some of the other disciples actually didn't have as much faith as Thomas did. Thomas at least expressed his doubt and verbalized his desire for evidence. What may have seemed like faith in some of the others, may have been a mask hiding their own doubts. We have to give Thomas credit for expressing his doubts and not being afraid of what he would find regardless of which way his investigation went.

We should never be afraid of wanting evidence. Granted, we may not always be able to get our hands on every piece of evidence we would like. But God is not afraid of our questions. And history has not yet revealed any evidence to contradict the biblical record of Christianity. So don't be afraid of asking for evidence.

Doubt Draws Us Back to Christ

Eight days after Jesus first appeared to the disciples, He came to them again. And this time Thomas was with them (verse 26). Perhaps Thomas purposed to stick closer to the group than he had done at first so he would not miss Jesus if He appeared to them again.

In our quest for answers and evidence, we ultimately must come in contact with a person—the Lord Jesus Christ. Christianity is not about doctrines and creeds. Christianity is about Christ. If we examine the right evidence, what we will find is Christ—not just answers. That's what happened to Thomas. In his search for evidence, he found Christ.

Sometimes it is too easy to get completely wrapped up in what we don't know, what we don't have answers for. In truth, the things we usually have questions about represent just a small minority, a tiny percentage, of the things revealed to us in Scripture about God and our faith in Him. And we get hung up on those things, majoring in minors. Someone has said we need to believe our beliefs and doubt our doubts. That's not bad advice. If we do that, we won't welcome with open arms every doubt we have as if it were automatically accurate and correct. We will, instead, view our doubts with a measure of caution, even skepticism. We'll hold them at arm's length until we're sure they represent something to pursue evidence for. In doing so, we hold the giant of doubt at bay, keeping him under our control.

Doubt Deepens Our Faith

It's possible that Thomas never would have seen Jesus if he hadn't doubted. He might not have rejoined the disciples without the motivation of seeing for himself whether Jesus was alive. And because he doubted and pursued the evidence, he had an amazing testimony to share. He had touched Jesus' wounds with his own hands (verse 27). He had first-hand knowledge that the Jesus who died on the cross was the same Jesus who had come back from the grave.

Honest doubts have the potential for building an indestructible faith if you will follow those doubts. Just as Jacob wrestled with the angel in Genesis 32:24 and came out of that experience a changed person, so your own doubts can cause you to come out stronger and more resilient in your faith. I have heard more than one person say that as they began to search for evidence, they found something they weren't expecting—a deeper relationship with God. They say, "I don't even care about the answers anymore. I've found the Lord in a whole new way."

Don't be surprised if you discover more than answers when you begin to confront your doubts about your faith.

Doubt Defines Our Faith

Somebody has said that "there is more faith in one doubt than in half the creeds." That means when we follow a doubt all the way through to the resolution of it in our heart, we can say with Thomas, "My Lord and my God!" (verse 28) That is one of the greatest professions of faith in all of the Bible, and it came on the heels of one man's doubts. Thomas' faith was defined like never before when he followed his doubts to their conclusion.

Some people are so steeped in the facts of Christianity that their faith has grown cold. They sort of keep it in reserve, like canned vegetables stored up for winter eating. When a doubt comes, they're forced to get their faith off the shelf and redefine it to make sure of what they believe. That is a positive thing when it happens.

FIGHTING THE GIANT OF DOUBT
Admit Your Doubts Personally

This is not always easy to do. You're probably not going to be inclined to go to prayer meetings and stand up and give testimony to your doubts—especially while everybody else is testifying to how great his or her walk with the Lord is going. But honesty is where

it starts. You don't have to announce your doubts to the Church, but you do need to verbalize them carefully to yourself. And perhaps even to a trusted friend or mentor in the faith, or your pastor. Separating what you're not sure about from what you are sure about is step number one.

Articulate Your Doubts Clearly

If you don't do this, Satan will grab the opportunity to convince you that you're just a doubter who can't believe anything. That's not true. If you're a Christian, you already believe a significant number of things with conviction. Be clear about the specific things you have questions about. Do you doubt the accuracy of the Bible? The reality of the Resurrection? The existence of heaven or hell? That there's only one way to God through Christ?

And why do you doubt? Have you been influenced by a book? A professor? Another believer? A non-believer? Identifying your doubts and their source will help you understand what you need answers for and why.

Acknowledge Your Doubts Prayerfully

Here is the most important point I want to make about fighting the giant of doubt: You must turn your doubts into prayers to God. Think of the people in the Old Testament whom God greatly used who had doubts when they heard His plans for them—Sarah, Moses, Gideon, and Jeremiah just to name a few. These people were approached by God Himself, and they still doubted! And God knew their doubts just as He knows yours and mine. We don't turn our doubts into prayers to God in order to inform God of our doubts. We tell God in order to verbalize what we are thinking and feeling about our faith. That makes it more understandable to us as we try to figure out what is going on in our lives.

Go to God with your doubts. He is waiting to hear from you.

Analyze the Evidence Diligently

It's one thing to sit back and entertain your doubts and wonder what the answers are. It's another thing to take responsibility for finding the answers and searching diligently for them. Sure, it takes some effort to do so. But the answers are there for most of the questions we have about the faith. You and I are not the first persons to have had the doubt we are having ("There is nothing new under the sun." Ecclesiastes 1:9). Many brilliant Christian scholars have tackled the great questions of the faith and produced mountains of answers

and evidence. If you don't know where to look, ask your pastor or mentor in the faith. Part of the responsibility that goes along with having questions is being willing to seek out the answers.

Accept the Limitations Humbly

1. Accept Your Limitations

    The more I study, the more I discover I don't know—and I study all the time! I continually pray that God would give me greater capacity to learn and know about Him. But I accept the fact that I will never know it all—and so should you. There are definite limitations to what we have the capacity and intelligence to know. So work as hard as you can, but accept your limitations.

2. Accept the Bible's Limitations

    Here is what I mean by this: Everything in the Bible is true, but not all truth is in the Bible. The Bible is not an encyclopedia or textbook containing the answer to every question in the world. That is not why it was given to us by God. But here is the most important thing to remember: The Bible has everything you need to know in order to know God and receive eternal life through faith in His Son. If you have other questions which are answered in the Bible, all the better. But if the Bible doesn't have the answers, don't doubt the answers the Bible does have.

Adjust to the Universe's Complexity

There is so much about the universe and the God who made it that we simply do not know. The bottom line is that we will never understand God and all of His ways. We are not supposed to. If we could, we would be like Him (and the last people who aspired to that goal got all of us in a lot of trouble, Genesis 3:5).

So we need to be reconciled to our place in the grand scheme of things. God's purposes, and what He has revealed to us of them, are moving ahead on His timetable. And He has told us what we need to know to make sure we are safely on board. As for what we don't know, use your doubts as assets, as tools to draw you closer to the truth. Put the giant of doubt in its place by solidifying your place in the faith.

PERSONAL QUESTIONS

1. Read Matthew 11:3.

   a. How did John the Baptist face his doubts?

   b. John had questions even after doing and witnessing what?
      (See Matthew 3:16-17.)

2. Read John 20:24-29.

   a. Why did Thomas question the Lord's resurrection? (verse 24)

   b. Has isolation ever led you to doubt the Word of God? Explain.

   c. What did Thomas demand in verse 25? Is it wrong to demand
      evidence or to look further into something when we doubt?
      Why or why not?

   d. What did Thomas' doubt lead him to? (verse 26)

   e. When Jesus came to the disciples again, what did He ask of
      Thomas? (verse 27)

f. How did Thomas respond in verse 28?

g. Like Thomas, has your doubt ever led you to further investigate the Bible? Did you find answers to your questions in the Word?

h. Have you found that verbalizing your doubts has led you to the answers you needed?

i. If you've faced doubt, what do you think was the ultimate reason? Who or what caused the doubt?

j. Describe a time when prayer helped you overcome your doubts in the Word.

k. Rather than entertaining our doubts and wondering what the answers are, what can we do instead?

l. Will we ever know everything about God and His Word? Why or why not?

1. Read John 20:24-29 together.

   a. What did Thomas say to the other disciples after they had seen the Lord? (verse 25) Where was he the first time Jesus appeared to them? (verse 24)

   b. What type of person was Thomas, as evidenced in John 11:16 and 14:5?

   c. What can happen to those who live in isolation, who are ill, or who feel discouraged when it comes to doubt? Discuss the saying "Our souls and our bodies live so close together, they catch each other's diseases."

   d. Was it wrong that Thomas demanded evidence? What did it lead him to do? (verses 26-27)

   e. Discuss what searching for evidence can do for our faith.

f. Who else wrestled with his faith in Genesis 32:24?

g. How did Thomas respond when he discovered Christ was alive? (verse 28)

2. Do any of you have doubts that need admitting? If comfortable, share with the group your concerns.

a. Discuss why it is important to turn our doubts into prayers. What is the purpose?

b. Does the Bible have answers to all our questions? What answers does the Bible give us?

c. If applicable, share how your research and study of the Word helped dissolve your doubts about your faith.

There are a couple of incidents in the Bible where people were without doubt about the status of a man, only to be proven completely wrong! When Joseph's torn tunic was brought before his father, Jacob said, "Without doubt Joseph is torn to pieces" (Genesis 37:33). Little did he know that Joseph was not only alive and would become a great leader, but that he would see his son again one day. And when the apostle Paul was bitten by a viper, the natives said, "No doubt this man is a murderer, whom, though he has escaped the sea, yet justice does not allow to live" (Acts 28:3-4). Little did they know that he was one of the greatest men to ever walk the earth!

SLAYING THE GIANT OF PROCRASTINATION

Acts 24:22-27

In this lesson we explore the dangers of failing to act on what we know.

OUTLINE

Truth be told, we all *know* more than we *do*. Sometimes we have good reasons for our inaction, but often it's because of laziness—it's human nature to put things off. The cost of procrastination is what we would have gained had we taken the opportunity before us.

I.   **Procrastination Robs You of Opportunities of Service**

II. **Procrastination Robs You of the Opportunity to Be Successful**

III. **Procrastination Robs You of the Opportunity of Salvation**
   A. The Identity of the Procrastinator
   B. The Instruction of the Procrastinator
   C. The Impact on the Procrastinator
   D. The Intention of the Procrastinator

IV. **Conclusion: Two Things**
   A. Procrastination Does Not Take Into Account the Uncertainty of Life
   B. Procrastination Does Not Take Into Account the Uniqueness of Conviction

Years ago, a very famous preacher surveyed the Bible to discover the most important words in Scripture. For instance, he wanted to find the saddest word in the Bible, the happiest word, and the most emotional word—along with a long list of additional words which were the superlatives in their category. When he came to the most dangerous word in the Bible, you might be surprised to know what he chose: *tomorrow*. That's right— *tomorrow*. *Tomorrow* is the most dangerous word because of its ability to rob dreamers of their dreams. It has robbed students of their educational opportunities and fathers of their relationships with their children. More than anything, it has kept more people from coming to Christ and finding salvation than any other word in the dictionary.

Satan's favorite word is *tomorrow*. If he can get someone to keep putting off thinking about his salvation until tomorrow, he has them right where he wants them. He uses tomorrow like the owner of the gas station who put a sign up that said, "Free gas tomorrow." Every time you look at the sign, it puts you off one more day. *Today* is the word that is dear to the heart of God, as in "today is the day to be saved!" (2 Corinthians 6:2, GNT)

In this lesson we're going to meet the giant of procrastination. It was active in the life of a Roman official named Felix whose story we find in Acts 24:22-27. Felix, and his wife Drusilla, missed the opportunity for salvation because of procrastination. Through them we will discover the dangers of procrastination and how to defeat it.

PROCRASTINATION ROBS YOU OF OPPORTUNITIES OF SERVICE

Jesus was talking to some of His followers once about the cost of discipleship. The essence of His words to them was that life has a way of putting obstacles in the path of the one who would seek first the Kingdom of God (Luke 9:59-62). Things such as taking care of family and the requirements of vocation are legitimate responsibilities. Was Jesus saying we should ignore those things in order to follow Him?

Of course not. He was simply illustrating that it's always easy to think of lots of reasons why we "can't" respond to the call of God in our life. Once we take care of all those details, we think then we'll get serious about following Christ.

Matthew 26 relates one of the saddest stories in the New Testament of a missed opportunity that could never be retrieved. Jesus went into

the Garden of Gethsemane on the night of His betrayal and arrest. He took Peter, James, and John into the garden with Him. Three times Jesus went aside to pray and three times discovered that His three friends had fallen asleep. They couldn't have known the historical significance of what was happening at that moment. But we can be sure that later they would have given anything to replay the events of that night. They would have wanted to stay awake and watch and pray for their Lord in His hour of agony. But they let one of the most critical nights in history pass them by.

One day in heaven each of us will no doubt look back and realize critical moments and hours of decision which we let slip through our fingers because of procrastination. If you're like me, there are times when I sense the Lord's leading to reach out to a certain person. And then I get busy and fail to follow up on it, only to discover later that there was something difficult going on in that person's life. Because I put off the Lord's leading, I missed the opportunity to reach out and minister to that person. That's an awful feeling to live with.

I have a feeling that after reading this lesson on procrastination, the Lord will bring a person to mind—maybe more than one—whom you have been meaning to call or reach out to. Respond to Him as soon as He speaks to your heart. I'd rather you obey Him than finish reading this chapter! Don't let anything stand in the way of following His leading in matters of spiritual urgency, whether in your life or the life of another person. Life is too precious and the consequences too eternal to do anything less than obey when we have the chance.

Procrastination Robs You of the Opportunity to Be Successful

No one who is a practicing procrastinator succeeds at anything. Procrastination robs you of the opportunity to succeed. Charles Swindoll describes the effect of procrastination as if procrastination were human. He personifies procrastination in a most effective way:

> [Procrastination] comes out a winner every time. . . . He can outtalk any student when it comes to homework. He can outthink any executive when it comes to correspondence. He can outwork any homemaker when it comes to vacuuming or doing dishes. He can outlast any parent when it comes to discipline. He can outsmart any salesman when it comes to selling. He has one basic product and he centers all his energy toward that single goal: defeat. By the sheer genius of suggestion, he becomes the epitome of what he destroys: success.[1]

You see, if we cannot take action when it is thrust upon us, we are doomed to defeat and failure.

He was going to be all that a mortal should be
    To-morrow.
No one should be kinder or braver than he
    To-morrow.
A friend who was troubled and weary he knew,
Who'd be glad of a lift and who needed it, too;
On him he would call and see what he could do
    To-morrow.
Each morning he stacked up the letters he'd write
    To-morrow
And thought of the folks he would fill with delight
    To-morrow.
It was too bad, indeed, he was busy to-day,
And hadn't a minute to stop on his way;
More time he would have to give others, he'd say,
    To-morrow.
The greatest of workers this man would have been
    To-morrow.
The world would have known him had he ever seen
    To-morrow
But the fact is he died and faded from view,
And all that was left when his living was through
Was a mountain of things he intended to do
    To-morrow.[2]

Any businessman or salesman will tell you that the art of succeeding is knowing what to do and when to do it—and doing it at that moment. Thomas Huxley was not a spiritual man, but he did have it right when it came to understanding procrastination: "The most important result of all education is to make you do the thing you have to do, when it ought to be done, whether you like it or not. It is the first lesson that ought to be learned. And however early a man's training begins, it is probably the last lesson that he learns thoroughly." What is that lesson? To do the thing you have to do when it has to be done.

Most people keep some sort of "To Do" list where they write down the tasks and goals they have for the day or week. But how many people purposefully take the hardest, most distasteful task and move it directly to the top of the list? Rather than pushing it to the bottom of the list, the person who is willing to do the hardest job when it needs to be done is on the road to success.

All of these practical reasons for defeating procrastination are important on a day-to-day basis. But there is another reason for conquering procrastination that is far more important. Procrastination can keep you out of heaven.

Procrastination Robs You of the Opportunity of Salvation

Procrastination can keep you from becoming a Christian. That's what happened to two people we meet in Acts 24, Felix and Drusilla.

The Identity of the Procrastinator

Some background on these two individuals will help you understand their spiritual situation:

1. Antonius Felix
   Felix was Antonius Felix. Greek by birth, he gained his appointment as Roman procurator of Judea from his brother.

2. Drusilla
   Drusilla, Felix's wife, was one of three daughters of Herod Agrippa I. Felix induced her to leave her husband and marry him. Her father, Herod Agrippa I, was the one who murdered James, the brother of John, and tried to murder Peter as well (Acts 12). Her great-uncle, Herod Antipas, was the one who executed John the Baptist, and her great-grandfather, Herod the Great, was the one who ordered the murder of all the baby boys in Bethlehem in an attempt to eliminate Jesus. This was Drusilla's family heritage. Spiritually dark, to say the least.

The apostle Paul was brought before Felix on charges of sedition. When Paul spoke, it was not to defend himself but to proclaim the Gospel of Christ (verse 24). No matter where Paul went, he always had one mission—to declare the Gospel. When Paul began to speak, it was almost as if Felix had been brought before Paul instead of Paul having been brought before Felix.

The Instruction of the Procrastinator

Paul spoke to Felix and Drusilla about his faith in Christ, and about three further points: "righteousness, self-control, and the judgment to come" (verse 25). That sermon was well-suited to Paul's audience that day because Felix and Drusilla were definitely needy in all three areas. We've already established that they were unrighteous people. Their marriage was immoral and their backgrounds were filled with spiritual darkness. They no doubt felt quite uncomfortable at Paul's words.

Then Paul moved on to self-control, another foreign word to them. They were used to doing whatever they wanted, unencumbered by moral restraints of any kind. And then he concluded with the natural outcome of unrighteousness and lack of self-control—judgment. Paul told them there is a Judge sitting on a throne much larger than the throne of the procurator of Judea, even the throne of the emperor himself in Rome. Someday, Paul told them, they would stand before that Judge and He would call them to account for their sins. That must have been some sermon, one that Felix and Drusilla never imagined they would hear when they woke up that morning.

The Impact on the Procrastinator

Felix's response to Paul's sermon was something we don't see much in contemporary preaching: fear. But "Felix was afraid" as a result of what he had heard from Paul—he was "terrified" in the words of the old American Standard Version (verse 25). God had spoken mightily to Felix's heart, and he was overtaken by fear at the prospect of future judgment in light of his past and present life.

But then, at the very time when he could have had all of his fears relieved, Felix said that most dangerous of words (in a manner of speaking): "Tomorrow."

The Intention of the Procrastinator

Felix sent Paul away, saying he would call for him again at a more convenient time (verse 25). Felix procrastinated, didn't he? He put off life's most important, and sometimes most difficult, task—getting right with the God who created, and who will judge, us all. We don't know if Felix ever believed the Gospel of Christ or not. Given his initial response, we would say the likelihood was not good. Even if he did later, we do know that he passed up the first chance God gave him to be saved. He put off until a "convenient time" that which he should have grasped immediately. There is never a "convenient time" to be saved. The time to be saved is when God shows you your need. Who knows whether you will ever sense that need again?

CONCLUSION: TWO THINGS

Procrastination is dangerous in any arena, but nowhere is it more dangerous than in the realm of salvation.

Procrastination Does Not Take Into Account the Uncertainty of Life

First of all, procrastination gives us the impression that we are in control of tomorrow. It does not take into account the uncertainty of life. If we knew for certain that tomorrow would come, perhaps we could put off some things. But who knows what life holds past today, past this minute? No one (Proverbs 27:1).

Scripture uses eighteen different metaphors to remind us of the transitory nature of life. For instance, life is like a vapor, here one minute and gone the next. Who would try to build their future on a vapor? That would be a foolish prospect indeed. To assume we can put off until tomorrow that which we should do today is a prescription for remorse—possibly eternal remorse.

In his letter to the churches, James warns about the presumption of thinking we are in control of tomorrow. Life is a "vapor that appears for a little time and then vanishes away" (James 4:14).

Are you putting off until tomorrow a decision about your own salvation? Or a decision to begin walking as a committed disciple of Christ, laying aside the things of this world and living only for Him? Perhaps you hear the Gospel presented regularly in church or on the radio, and you keep telling yourself you need to respond and get things settled with God. If you are putting this off, you are building your future on a foundation of vapor. You do not know what tomorrow will bring. Today is the day for salvation.

But let's assume you have absolute control over tomorrow, that you know exactly how many days you have left to live. There is still a problem. You don't know whether conviction will ever touch your heart again.

Procrastination Does Not Take Into Account the Uniqueness of Conviction

I refer to the special times when God deals with each person as "defining moments." Every Christian can think back to the time he was saved and recognize the uniqueness of the situation. Something happened that day that had not happened the day before. The moment of your salvation was a unique event. God brought together all the factors and influences necessary in order for you to recognize your need for Him.

You may get a tomorrow, but there is no guarantee that when tomorrow comes, you will be convicted of your need for Christ. Just as it happened with Felix—he came under sincere conviction the day Paul preached to him—it happens to each of us. The danger is that we, like Felix, will ignore that conviction and put it off until a more "convenient time." The problem is that the convenient time may never come. You may never be convicted again of your need for salvation.

The prophet Isaiah said it best: "Seek the Lord while He may be found, call upon Him while He is near" (Isaiah 55:6). If you know the Lord can be found today, then today is the day you need to call upon Him—while He is near.

Procrastination is a giant that will rob you of opportunities for service and the opportunity to be successful. But most of all it will rob you of the opportunity to be saved. Don't put off doing anything that you know needs to be done today. You have no guarantees about tomorrow and no promise that the promptings you feel today will ever be there again. Whatever you do, don't procrastinate about being saved. Today may be the only chance you have.

Notes

1. Charles R. Swindall, "Growing Strong in the Seasons of Life" (Multnomah Press, Portland OR: 1983).

2. Edgar A. Guest, "To-morrow," *A Heap O'Livin'* (Reilly and Lee Company, Chicago: 1916).

1. What word must we beware of, especially when it comes to salvation?

2. What does 2 Corinthians 6:2 say about salvation?

3. In Luke 9:59-62, what does Jesus say about those who seek the Kingdom of God?

   a. Should we ignore our everyday tasks to follow Him?

   b. What, then, does Jesus mean?

4. What is true about procrastination when it comes to our success?

5. Read Acts 24:22-27.

   a. In verse 24, whom did Paul speak to concerning the Gospel of Christ?

   b. What three things did Paul mention about salvation to Felix and Drusilla? (verse 25)

   c. What was Felix's demeanor after he heard what Paul had to say? What was his response? (verse 25)

6. According to James 4:14, what is the reality of tomorrow? What image is life compared to?

   a. Is there any person who knows what life holds tomorrow? (Proverbs 27:1)

   b. Does this mean we should never make plans for tomorrow? Explain.

   c. Is there a decision or task you are putting off? What is stopping you from making the decision or accomplishing the task today?

GROUP QUESTIONS

1. Review Luke 9:59-62.

   a. What does Jesus say about following Him in verse 62? Does this mean we shouldn't work or take care of loved ones or maintain our responsibilities?

   b. What does this have to do with procrastination and making excuses?

2. Share about a time when procrastination robbed you of your success, whether in school, at home, at work, etc.

3. Read Acts 24:22-27 as a group.

   a. Discuss Felix and Drusilla's background to better understand their spiritual lives.

   b. What things did Paul speak to Felix and Drusilla about regarding faith? (verse 25)

   c. What word does the American Standard Version use in verse 25 to describe Felix's state of emotions?

   d. What did Felix ask of Paul? (verse 25) What is dangerous about putting salvation, and most other things, off until a "convenient time"?

   e. What do we learn about life from James 4:14?

f. What does Isaiah 55:6 encourage us to do?

g. Is there anyone you know, a relative or friend, who has not
received Christ as Savior? What is holding that person back?
How can you encourage that person to accept Christ today?

DID YOU KNOW?

Isn't it interesting how we hate to wait for other people and events;
but when it comes to our own actions, we wait as long as possible?
Just think about Abraham and Sarah. They were so discontent
waiting for the Lord to give them a child that Sarah gave Abraham
her servant Hagar to bear him one instead (Genesis 16:3). Yet Jonah
was perfectly content with procrastinating and disobeying God's
instruction to preach repentance to Nineveh. It took three days in a
fish to straighten him out (Jonah 1:17)!

SLAYING THE GIANT OF FAILURE

2 Corinthians 4:7-18

*In this lesson we learn how failure can be made
a stepping-stone to success.*

OUTLINE

There is a world of difference between "You're a failure!" and
"You failed." The former speaks to our character, the latter to one
specific event in life. Just because we fail one or many times, it does
not mean we have been disqualified from the race to succeed.

I. Facing the Giant of Failure
    A. Facing the Reality of Failure
    B. Facing the Reason for Failure
    C. Facing the Result of Failure

II. Fighting the Giant of Failure
    A. Acknowledge Your Failure
    B. Accept God's Forgiveness
    C. Apply the Lessons of Failure Toward Success
    D. Accept Failure as a Fact of Life, Not a Way of Life
    E. Arise From Failure and Start Again
    F. Avoid Judging Failure in Others

I t's one thing when you and I have an experience of failure in our private lives. Our failure is known only to a small circle of friends and family. But it's a totally different thing when you're the most important political leader in the world and your every move is reported live by the news media around the world. Such was the case when the late President George H. W. Bush became ill and vomited at a state dinner in Japan—which included the Prime Minister of Japan in the "effects" of his ill health.

Granted, that probably doesn't qualify as a personal failure. We don't normally hold people responsible for illnesses they have no control over. But that is probably not how President George H. W. Bush felt. He probably felt himself a failure when his embarrassing moment in Japan took place. Indeed, when he had lain down on the carpet in order to be attended to by his physician, he moaned, "Just roll me under the table until dinner is over." At least his "failure" didn't cloud his sense of humor.

What we traditionally think of as failure happened in 1957 when the Ford Motor Company released to the public what it called "the car of the decade"—the Edsel. It was supposed to be the most dramatic advance in engineering and design since the invention of the automobile a half-century earlier. Sadly, it turned out to be the biggest bomb in the history of the automotive industry. It was, to put it mildly, a colossal failure. Ford's best efforts to succeed turned out to be the worst effort in the company's history.

Life is filled with failure, whether presidential, corporate, or personal. The person who does not learn to manage failure, to defeat the giant of failure, will soon find himself buried under a mountain of disgrace and shame. But the person who learns to profit from failure will find himself climbing ever higher mountains of accomplishment. What the giant of failure means to trip you with can turn out to be a ticket to the future—but only if we understand failure from God's perspective.

FACING THE GIANT OF FAILURE

In 1988, the United Technologies Corporation published an ad in *The Wall Street Journal* reminding us of our failures. The ad said,

You've failed many times, although you may not remember.
You fell down the first time you tried to walk.
You almost drowned the first time you tried to swim.
Did you hit the ball the first time you swung a bat?
Heavy hitters, the ones who hit the most home runs,
    also strike out a lot.

R. H. Macy failed seven times before his store in New York caught on.

English novelist John Creasey got 733 rejection slips before he published 564 books.

Babe Ruth struck out 1,330 times, but he also hit 714 home runs.

Don't worry about failure.

Worry about the chances you miss when you don't even try.

The first thing every person needs to do is face not the possibility of failure but the reality of failure.

Facing the Reality of Failure

Paul introduces the likelihood of failure in his own life in an interesting way (2 Corinthians 4:7-9). He talks about the treasure we have in "earthen vessels." What does he mean? The treasure is the Gospel, and the earthen vessels are our frail and fragile human bodies. God has entrusted the priceless treasure of His Gospel to be kept safe in the bodies of human beings.

What happens to human bodies? They are "hard-pressed . . . perplexed . . . persecuted . . . struck down," but never totally defeated. Though never knocked out, we are knocked down continually in life. In other words, we fail a lot. The fact of failure is factored into our humanity. It comes with the package.

In a book titled *The Incomplete Book of Failures*, author Stephen Pile lists some of the failures associated with people you thought always did everything successfully:

- An expert said of famous football coach Vince Lombardi, "He possesses minimal football knowledge. Lacks motivation."

- Beethoven handled the violin awkwardly and preferred playing his own compositions instead of improving his technique. His teacher called him hopeless as a composer.

- Walt Disney was fired by a newspaper editor for lack of ideas. He went bankrupt several times before he built Disneyland.

- Thomas Edison's teacher said he was too stupid to learn anything.

- Albert Einstein did not speak until he was four years old, and couldn't read until he was seven. His teacher described him as "mentally slow, unsociable and adrift forever in his foolish dreams." He was expelled and refused admittance to the Zurich Polytechnic School.

- F. W. Woolworth's employers at the dry goods store where he worked said he didn't have enough sense to wait on the customers.

- Henry Ford failed and went broke five times before he finally succeeded.
- Winston Churchill failed the sixth grade. He did not become Prime Minister of England until he was 62 and only after a lifetime of setbacks and failures.

There are many more examples which could be cited. It is true that many people who succeed significantly have a string of failures somewhere in their past.

God is not surprised by our failure. Indeed, He expects it because He knows who we are (Psalm 103:13-14). We saw in our last lesson that the disciples failed to stay awake and watch and pray with Jesus in the Garden of Gethsemane. Jesus' conclusion was, "The spirit indeed is willing, but the flesh is weak" (Matthew 26:41). God knows our propensity to fail and so understands our requests when we come to Him in times of failure (Hebrews 4:15-16).

The famous Scottish preacher Alexander Whyte described spiritual growth like this: "Spiritual growth is the saints falling down and getting up, falling down and getting up, falling down and getting up, all the way to heaven." If you are like me, you can identify with that!

Facing the Reason for Failure

Why does God allow failure in our life? What good purpose does it serve? Second Corinthians 4:17 and 18 reveal four reasons for failure:

1. We Fail Now So That We Might Succeed Later

   Affliction is for now; glory is for the future. The Bible tells us that if we are going to reign with the Lord, we are going to have to suffer with Him as well (Romans 8:17). Glory is best appreciated by those who have first experienced the lack of it.

2. We Fail in the Incidental So That We Might Succeed in the Important

   Paul talks about "light affliction" and "weight of glory." The things that happen to us now, in light of eternity, are not as "heavy" as we think they are.

3. We Fail in the Temporary So That We Might Succeed in the Eternal

   Paul talks about that which is for the moment and contrasts it with that which is eternal. Our failures in time prepare us for "success" in eternity.

4. We Fail Outwardly So That We Might Succeed Inwardly

   God cares far less about our outward success than He does our inward success. While we are wrapped up in what we do,

God is focused on who we are. Our goal is to learn to focus on the unseen, not the seen things—just as God does. Failure helps us do that.

Peter Marshall said, "It is better to fail in a cause that will ultimately succeed than to succeed in a cause that will ultimately fail." Though our earthen vessels may fail, the treasure we carry in them will not. We may fail on the way to heaven, but we will get there in Christ.

Facing the Result of Failure

I love verse 16: "We do not lose heart." Why don't we lose heart? Because in spite of all the failure we experience year after year in our lives, "the inward man is being renewed day by day." On a daily basis, God is transforming our inner man. We do not put our emphasis and priority on succeeding in the outward realm because that world is perishing. It is the inner man and the inward world that God is refreshing and renewing day by day.

Given these tremendous truths, the reality is that failure is not fun. It is painful and discouraging when it happens. And that's when the giant of discouragement is ready to pounce on us, to convince us to throw in the towel. How do we fight this giant when he comes around?

FIGHTING THE GIANT OF FAILURE

Acknowledge Your Failure

Overcoming failure—and profiting from it—begins with us. Former President Harry Truman knew how to honestly evaluate things, even his own life. When asked if he was popular as a child in school, he replied, "No. I was never popular. The popular boys were the ones who were good at games and had big fists. I was never like that. Without my glasses, I was blind as a bat, and to tell the truth, I was kind of a sissy. If there was any chance of getting into a fight, I took off. I guess that's why I'm here today." In modern language, he "failed" at being popular, but he wasn't afraid to admit it.

Sometimes we hesitate to admit our failure because we think of it like confessing sin. All sin is a failure of some sort, but not all failure is sin. So don't be afraid to admit it when you fail.

Accept God's Forgiveness

If our failure is due to sin, the only way to overcome its effects is to confess it to God and receive His forgiveness. The clear testimony of Scripture is that God is a forgiving God. He does not condone our sinful failures, but neither does He hold them against us if we want to be forgiven for them (Psalm 103:10; 1 John 1:9).

Apply the Lessons of Failure Toward Success

We should never accept failure as the final judgment or assessment of our potential. If we did that, we would never move beyond our first failure. We must learn to use failure as a resource, as an opportunity. An assistant to Thomas Edison tried to console him after a string of failed experiments had produced no results. "Oh, we have lots of results," Edison said. "We know 700 things that won't work!" John Keates, an English author, once wrote, "Failure is in a sense the highway to success, inasmuch as every discovery of what is false leads us to seek earnestly after what is true, and every fresh experience points out some form of error which we shall afterward carefully avoid."

By studying our failures, we will discover what we are doing wrong, which can only lead us more quickly to what to do right.

Accept Failure as a Fact of Life, Not a Way of Life

Failure is an event, not a person; failure is something that happens, not someone you become. We carelessly use the phrase, "I'm a failure," so frequently that we begin to believe it. A person can have hundreds and hundreds of failures in his life and still be a success. Or, if he allows just a few failures to overcome him, he could be on the road to characterizing himself as a failure.

Think about Peter's failure to identify with the Lord Jesus on the night of His arrest. And then think about him preaching with fire at Pentecost in the opening of the book of Acts. Peter failed, but he wasn't a failure.

Arise From Failure and Start Again

The temptation when we fail is to wallow in self-pity, to sulk, to feel sorry for ourselves (a sure sign of the influence of the giant of failure). The best thing you can do is stand up, brush yourself off, and start moving forward again.

One of my favorite characters in Scripture is Jonah. You know his story, how God told him to go one way (east to Nineveh) and he went the other (west toward Spain). Jonah failed miserably in his role and responsibility as a prophet. Yet after he had come back to the Lord, God gave him a second chance (Jonah 3:1-2). He sent him again to Nineveh to preach, and 120,000 people repented before God. It was one of the greatest responses to the Word of God recorded in history. And this from a man who just a short time previously had failed miserably.

Sometimes when you try to start over, people will say, "You're a failure." That's the enemy talking—don't listen. You listen to God who wants you to succeed. If you are right with Him, He will be right with you.

Avoid Judging Failure in Others

Just as others might judge us, we must be on guard against judging others as a failure. We'll close this lesson by looking at the examples of two people who were judged by others as failures, but whom God saw as successes.

1. The Rich Man and the Beggar

   In Luke 16, the story of the rich man and Lazarus reveals two opposite individuals. Outwardly the rich man was the success and Lazarus the failure. But God's perspective was the opposite. The rich man ended up in agony, and Lazarus ended up being comforted in Paradise. If we had seen the two before knowing God's evaluation, would we have been quick to judge? God's values are often very different than ours.

2. A Pharisee and a Tax Collector

   In Luke 18, we have the story of a Pharisee and a tax collector. The Pharisee was the epitome of success within first-century Judaism, and the tax collector one of the most despised men in town. But when they went to the temple to pray, their true success and failure became obvious. The Pharisee was proud and arrogant, the tax collector humble and repentant. Which would we have chosen as the success and which the failure?

These stories warn us to beware of judging others who appear to us to be failures. The Man who, from the world's point of view, was a great failure turned out to be the Man God exalted and honored by raising Him from the dead and seating Him at the right hand of the throne of God. Don't fall into the trap of thinking you are a failure when you fail. Defeat the giant of failure by striving to receive Jesus' final words about your life: "Well done, good and faithful servant."

PERSONAL QUESTIONS

1. Read 2 Corinthians 4:7-18.

   a. What has God entrusted to our bodies (earthen vessels)? (verse 7) What happens to our earthly bodies according to verses 8-9?

   b. Recall some of the failures listed in the section "Facing the Reality of Failure." What is true of those who succeed?

   c. How should we face failure according to verse 16?

   d. What four reasons for failure do verses 17-18 reveal? What are we to focus on—the things which are seen or the things which are unseen—and why?

   e. Why do you think it is common to see only the outward appearance of a person rather than the inward? Have you ever found yourself doing so? Why?

   f. After we acknowledge our failure, what are we told to do in 1 John 1:9? What two things does God do for us?

   g. Is "failure" someone we become or something that happens to us? Like Peter and Jonah, how can you move past your failures and start again?

2. In the story of the Pharisee and tax collector, what did Jesus say will happen to those who exalt themselves? (Luke 18:14)

   a. What will happen to those who humble themselves?

   b. How can the truth of this verse encourage you the next time you fail?

1. Review 2 Corinthians 4:7-18.

   a. What is the first thing we need to face—the possibility of failure or the reality of it?

   b. Recall what Paul says about our bodies in verses 8-9. Though knocked down continually, what will never happen to us?

   c. What is the precursor for success in many cases? Share, if applicable, how failure led to success in a certain area of your life.

   d. Review the four reasons we have for failure. Why do we fail in our temporary, outward lives?

   e. What does God care more about—our outward success or our inward success? Why?

   f. According to verse 16, why should we not lose heart when we fail?

2. When we fail, we don't necessarily sin—but when we sin, we in turn fail. When we come to God with our sins, what is His response? (Psalm 103:10; 1 John 1:9)

3. Recall the story of Jonah. After he experienced failure, what happened when he came back to God? (Jonah 3:1-2)

4. Whom did God see as successful—the rich man or the beggar, the Pharisee or the tax collector? Why?

5. Discuss why it is important not to judge others when they fail.

DID YOU KNOW?

Failure is often a momentary judgment that is projected upon a person or situation. Surely many thought that Noah was a failure as he tirelessly built an ark for a flood that was not apparent. But time proved Noah a success (Genesis 7:23). Samson would be considered a failure if his life had stopped after he was betrayed by Delilah. But in his blind and weakened state, God gave Samson one last triumph (Judges 16:30). Likewise, many of the followers of Jesus considered Him a failure when He was crucified and died (Luke 24:21). Yet once again, time proved Jesus the victor (Mark 16:19)!

SLAYING THE GIANT OF JEALOUSY

Selected Scriptures

*In this lesson we learn about jealousy
in order to avoid its traps.*

OUTLINE

Jealousy has two sides—a positive and a negative. When we are jealous *for* another, we have their best interests at heart. When we're jealous *of* another, we're embarking on a selfish journey that can only end in travail. Self-centered jealousy is a sin to be avoided.

I. **Jealousy Travels in Circles**
   A. Jealousy Travels in Proprietary Circles
   B. Jealousy Travels in Power Circles
   C. Jealousy Travels in Performance Circles
   D. Jealousy Travels in Professional Circles
   E. Jealousy Travels in Personal Circles

II. **The Characteristics of Jealousy**
   A. Jealousy Destroys Others
   B. Jealousy Destroys Ourselves

III. **Facing the Giant of Jealousy**
   A. Renounce Jealousy as Sin
   B. Remember Your Rival in Prayer
   C. Reaffirm God's Goodness to You
   D. Rekindle God's Love in Your Heart

An ancient Greek legend sets the stage for our final lesson in which we confront and learn to defeat the giant of jealousy. It seems a young Greek athlete ran in a race and placed second. In honor of the winner, his village erected a large statue in the town square. Envy and jealousy attacked the runner who came in second to the degree that he made plans to destroy the statue. Each night, under cover of darkness, he went out and chipped away at the foundation of the statue, expecting it to fall on its own some day. One night, however, he chipped too much. The statue's weakened base began to crack until it popped. The huge marble statue came down upon the disgruntled athlete. He died under the crushing weight of the one he had come to hate.

The truth is, he died long before the statue fell on him. In giving up his heart to envy and jealousy, he had ceased to live for himself. He became a slave to the giant of jealousy. His heart had become a picture of the Greek word *envy*, which means "to boil within."

Shakespeare called jealousy the green sickness. To be jealous means to strike out at what somebody else is or what somebody else has. Whereas Scripture says that we are to rejoice with those who rejoice and weep with those who weep, the jealous person does the opposite. He rejoices when others weep, and weeps when others rejoice. Another's setback is his opportunity for advancement; another's sorrow is his chance to gain the ascendancy. When the person of whom he is jealous is successful, he turns green with envy. When that person experiences failure, he flushes with the chance to make up lost ground.

Jealousy can eat away at one's insides as Proverbs suggests (Proverbs 14:30). No giant is more destructive to self and to relationships than the giant of jealousy and envy. To close our study without conquering this giant would leave one vulnerable. Why leave alive the one giant that can erode the peace and joy gained by conquering all of the others?

JEALOUSY TRAVELS IN CIRCLES

Jealousy makes its way through a number of networks or circles in which we each travel. To be aware of its favorite pathways is to be forearmed against its power.

Jealousy Travels in Proprietary Circles

Jealousy is found in the arena of possessions and wealth. For instance, Genesis 26:13-14 describes the wealth Isaac accumulated and how the Philistines "envied him." Isaac's possessions are

mentioned three times, so we know he had accumulated quite a lot. And though the Philistines were wealthy seafaring traders, they still envied what Isaac had. Jealousy can easily get a foothold among the wealthy. It's easy to want just a little bit more than we already have.

To be sure, it is possible to have wealth and not envy what anyone else has. God has blessed many Christians with significant wealth, and many of them have learned to live with gratitude toward God instead of envy toward others. But generally speaking, jealousy and envy have an easy time stirring up trouble in the circles of the wealthy.

Jealousy Travels in Power Circles

Not only does wealth envy wealth, but power envies power. Miriam and Aaron were jealous of Moses' power and position among the people (Numbers 12), as was Korah (Numbers 16). In the books of Kings and Chronicles we read story after story of kings who usurped the power of other kings, often by criminal and traitorous acts, only to have the same thing happen to them once they reached the pinnacle of power. History is littered with the ruins of nations whose leaders, motivated by jealousy and envy, led them to war.

In the four Gospels and the book of Acts, we read that the Jewish leaders were jealous of Jesus' power and influence among the people, and later that of His apostles. They crucified Jesus and threw His apostles into jail—and worse (Acts 7:54–8:1)—in part on the basis of jealousy and fear that their own power base was eroding.

Power circles can be a breeding ground for jealousy in the business world—and even in the Church. Whose organization is biggest? Who's getting the most media attention? Who has the most employees? Power can promote jealousy among those who have it.

Jealousy Travels in Performance Circles

If there is a circle where Christians are most vulnerable, this is probably it—individually and corporately. Remember the story in the Old Testament of Saul and David? David became the young hero in Israel after he slew the Philistine giant, Goliath. The green sickness of jealousy began to grow in Saul's heart as he saw the hearts of Israel go out to David. Saul spent the rest of his life trying to eliminate the object of his jealousy, tracking David all over the Judean wilderness trying to kill him. He remained a captive to his jealousy until he died.

The local church, I am ashamed to say, is a place where jealousy lurks, waiting for a chance to attack. Perhaps it is because the church is a "volunteer" organization. People give their money and volunteer their time and, as a result, feel they are entitled to certain things—

sing a solo, chair a committee, receive recognition when those roles, responsibilities, and recognition are given to others. How subtle and insidious the enemy is to stir up jealousy and envy in our midst, and how naïve we are to succumb to it!

The Church of Jesus Christ is the last place the giant of jealousy should ever find a home because grace and love can infect us, making us impervious to envy's attacks.

Jealousy Travels in Professional Circles

An amazing example of envy occurred once when Paul was incarcerated for preaching the Gospel. While he was in jail, others were taking advantage of his imprisonment and preaching the Gospel, hoping to gain for themselves some of the attention Paul had received (Philippians 1:15-16). And Paul had an interesting response. He said that even though others were preaching the Gospel using envy as a motive (some were also preaching from proper motives), he took comfort knowing that the Gospel was being proclaimed. He didn't respond angrily or out of resentment, which would have revealed jealousy in his own life—that others were gathering to themselves "fame" which was rightly his. He was content to sit in his jail cell and allow God to sort out the motives in men's hearts. He was simply happy that the Gospel was being preached.

Jealousy Travels in Personal Circles

We may not be wealthy or powerful, have roles to perform or other professionals to compete with—but we are all people. And jealousy shows up most often in the relationships we have with other people just like ourselves. This is probably where we see it the most and certainly where we see it the most in the Bible. In the Old Testament, Cain was jealous of Abel, Ishmael was jealous of Isaac, and Jacob and Esau were jealous of each other. And Joseph's brothers were so envious of him that they sold him into slavery. In the New Testament, the prodigal son story gives us a sad illustration of jealousy (Luke 15:11-32). We are often so involved in focusing on the prodigal and his return to the father that we miss the burning jealousy of the older brother. He was incensed that his father had never rewarded him for his faithfulness and obedience, and here the prodigal was being welcomed home like a hero. His jealousy had blinded his eyes to his own Pharisee-like misunderstanding of love and grace.

When jealousy comes in the front door, love goes out the back door. The two cannot coexist in the same person. Rest assured that if you are struggling with jealousy, you are also struggling with love.

Before looking at the characteristics of jealousy, it is important to remember that jealousy will most likely raise its head in the circles in which one travels. As a pastor and preacher, I am not jealous of plumbers, professional wrestlers, painters, or bank presidents, as much as I admire and respect what they do. My temptations with jealousy are going to arise in the circles in which I travel, and they will most often for you as well.

This old fable well illustrates my point: The devil was crossing the Libyan Desert when he came across a group of junior devils who were tempting a holy man. They tried to tempt him with the flesh, with doubts, with fear, with lies—nothing they did could induce the holy man to sin. The devil asked the juniors to step aside so that he might show them how to reach the old man. The devil leaned forward and whispered in the man's ear, "Have you heard the news? Your brother has just been made Bishop of Alexandria." With that, a cloud of jealousy covered the now-not-so-holy man's face—and the devil had him.

Be careful about becoming jealous in the circles in which you travel.

THE CHARACTERISTICS OF JEALOUSY

Above all else, jealousy always does two things.

Jealousy Destroys Others

Cain killed Abel. Saul tried to kill David. Herod killed babies so King Jesus wouldn't come to power in his realm. Envy and jealousy lead people to do unthinkable things to others. I recall reading a story about a mother who killed a teenaged girl who was competing for a cheerleading spot that the woman wanted her daughter to win. Killing a child over jealousy regarding a cheerleading position!

But lest we presume ourselves immune from such acts, we need only remember the jealous thoughts we ourselves have had. Acts of jealousy begin with thoughts of jealousy.

Jealousy Destroys Ourselves

Remember in the book of Esther how Haman was hanged on the scaffold he had built for the object of his jealousy? And how those who threw Daniel in the lions' den were the ones consumed? And how Joseph's brothers ended up begging for food from the object of their jealousy? And how Saul was consumed by his jealousy while David was content with his psalms? The jealous person is the one who ultimately suffers the most.

There is little argument that jealousy and envy are destructive attitudes. The question is, how do we conquer them?

FACING THE GIANT OF JEALOUSY

Like many of the other giants we have covered in our study, jealousy falls into the category of personal choice. If we are jealous, it's not because we were born with it or caught it like a cold. Therefore, our strategy for conquering jealousy is based on what it is: a sinful choice we make.

Renounce Jealousy as Sin

We read in the Gospels that Jesus Christ was handed over and put to death because of envy (Matthew 27:18; Mark 15:10). Every time I begin to get comfortable accommodating jealousy and envy in my life, I need to remember how sinful they are—sinful enough to have caused the death of the sinless Son of God. If those responsible for the death of Christ did so on the basis of sinful envy, why is my envy any less sinful than theirs? It is not. Envy and jealousy are the same in every human heart—sinful choices that we choose to indulge in and nurture.

First and foremost, jealousy must be renounced as sin.

Remember Your Rival in Prayer

If you are jealous of another person, the best thing to do is pray for that person and thank God for their success or whatever it is you envy. A story is told about two famous preachers in London. F. B. Meyer was the older, established preacher and Charles Spurgeon was the younger, newer preacher in town. When Spurgeon became the toast of the town—he preached to tens of thousands on Sunday and the newspaper printed his sermons on the front page—Meyer began to envy him. But he immediately began to pray for his success. Soon, because of his partnership in prayer, Meyer was able to rejoice in the blessings of God upon Spurgeon. And his own church eventually benefited greatly from the upsurge in spiritual interest in London.

Pray for those for whom you feel the slightest twinge of envy.

Reaffirm God's Goodness to You

Here is something important I have learned about jealousy: It is almost always because we don't think God has been as good to us as we think He should have been. If we are jealous of another person, it is because we want the blessings God has given to him. We don't understand why He has blessed them and not us, and we become jealous of what they have that we don't have. The quickest way to put an end to that kind of thinking is to take an inventory of our own blessings.

If we have anything at all, it is because we have been blessed. All we deserve is judgment. But all of us have far more than we deserve, and most of us have far more than we need. When we begin to thank God for all that He has blessed us with—stop right now and consider your blessings—it will be hard to continue in a jealous frame of mind toward another. In the purposes of God, how could we possibly be jealous of what He has done for another when He has done so much for us? Thanksgiving will douse the spark of jealousy and fan the flames of gratitude every time.

Rekindle God's Love in Your Heart

First Corinthians 13:4 holds the key to defeating the giant of jealousy: "Love does not envy." Where love is, envy cannot abide. If envy marches in the front door, love will sweep it out the back door. If jealousy sneaks in the back, love will usher it out the front. The house of love has no room for jealousy to even visit, much less take up residence.

Rekindle God's love by reading the Word and praying. Ask God to fill you with His Spirit whose fruit is love. Then act on those prayers by manifesting the love of God to any person toward whom you have felt envy or jealousy. Your walk must match your talk when it comes to love triumphing over jealousy.

My prayer for you as we conclude our study of spiritual giants is that Jesus Christ will be the spiritual giant in your life, filling you with thanksgiving, joy, and gratitude. When His love fills your heart, it will push out the jealousies and envies of life. And, you will have more victory over the giants of fear, discouragement, loneliness, worry, guilt, temptation, anger, resentment, doubt, procrastination, permanent failure, and jealousy. Let His Word abide in you, and you will walk in victory over every would-be giant you encounter.

PERSONAL QUESTIONS

1. Answer the following questions about jealousy.

   a. What does the Greek word *envy* mean?

   b. What does Proverbs 14:30 suggest about jealousy?

   c. Though the Philistines were wealthy, what did they feel toward Isaac? (Genesis 26:13-14)

   d. Is it possible to have wealth and not envy what others have? Do you know someone who embodies this trait?

   e. Who envied Moses according to Numbers 12 and 16? Why? Have you been witness to this type of jealousy in power circles? How did it get resolved?

   f. While Paul was imprisoned, what motive did others have for preaching the Gospel? How did Paul react? (Philippians 1:15-16)

   g. Where does jealousy most often show up in your life? Why do you think it is so easy to let jealousy toward others into our hearts?

   h. Who suffers more—those toward whom we are jealous or those of us who are jealous? Why?

2. Is jealousy something we are born with? First and foremost, jealousy must be renounced as what?

   a. What is the best thing we can do for those toward whom we are jealous?

   b. Using 1 Corinthians 13:4 as a guide, what are some steps you can take this week to remove jealousy from your own life?

1. Answer the following questions as a group.

   a. What effect can jealousy have on us physically? (Proverbs 14:30)

   b. Why were the Philistines jealous of Isaac? (Genesis 26:13-14) What does this reveal about the wealthy? Is this true of every person of wealth?

   c. What happened to Jesus and His disciples because of others' jealousy? (Acts 7:54-8:1)

   d. Discuss how jealousy might show up even within the local church.

   e. If applicable, share from your own experiences how jealousy affected your professional life. How did it affect Paul's ministry? (Review Philippians 1:15-16.)

   f. What does the story of the prodigal son reveal about jealousy in our personal lives?

2. What two things does jealousy always do? List them below and discuss.

   a. Jealousy destroys _____.

   b. Jealousy destroys _____.

3. What can we remember about envy based on Matthew 27:18 and Mark 15:10?

DID YOU KNOW?

The Ten Commandments cover many aspects on the topic of jealousy. Exodus 20:5 says that God is "a jealous God"; that is, He wants the desire, attention, and worship of His people to be where it needs to be—on Him. Thus we get the first and second commandments which admonish us to serve and bow down to no other god but God. The tenth commandment is built upon our sinful, jealous natures; it admonishes us not to covet those things that do not belong to us (Exodus 20:17). Instead, we are to continually give thanks to God for all the things that He has provided for us in our lives.

OVERCOMER

In *Overcomer*, Dr. David Jeremiah guides readers through the spiritual armor of the believer. He teaches us what it means to stand firm and overcome sin in this world filled with evil, reminding us that, as believers, we have everything we need to live a victorious life in Christ. Dr. Jeremiah explains that when we "put on" Christ, we can overcome the schemes and strategies of the evil one.

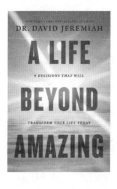

A LIFE BEYOND AMAZING

God has called us to more than just an ordinary life—He has called us to a life beyond amazing! In this book, Dr. Jeremiah shares God's strategy for change, challenging us to make nine important decisions—based on the fruit of the Spirit—that will transform our hearts and lives while on earth.

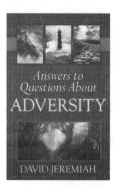

ANSWERS TO QUESTIONS ABOUT ADVERSITY

When more days than not are filled with hardships, we wonder, *Why is life so hard?* The Bible has answers for us if we would only look to its pages for help. But where do we turn? This question-and-answer book draws from the Word, answering many of our toughest questions about the adversities of life. How wonderful that God has the answers to our questions!

WHEN YOUR WORLD FALLS APART

Life can change in an instant. But when life turns upside down, God is there in our midst. He comforts, guides, encourages, and sustains. In this book, Dr. Jeremiah draws from his own experience and shares truths from the Psalms to comfort and strengthen us as we journey into the unknown, reminding us that God's grace is sufficient for every need.

Each of these resources was created from a teaching series by Dr. David Jeremiah. Contact Turning Point for more information about correlating materials.

For pricing information and ordering, contact us at

P.O. Box 3838
San Diego, CA 92163
(800) 947-1993
www.DavidJeremiah.org